Bits and Pieces II

Using Fraction Operations

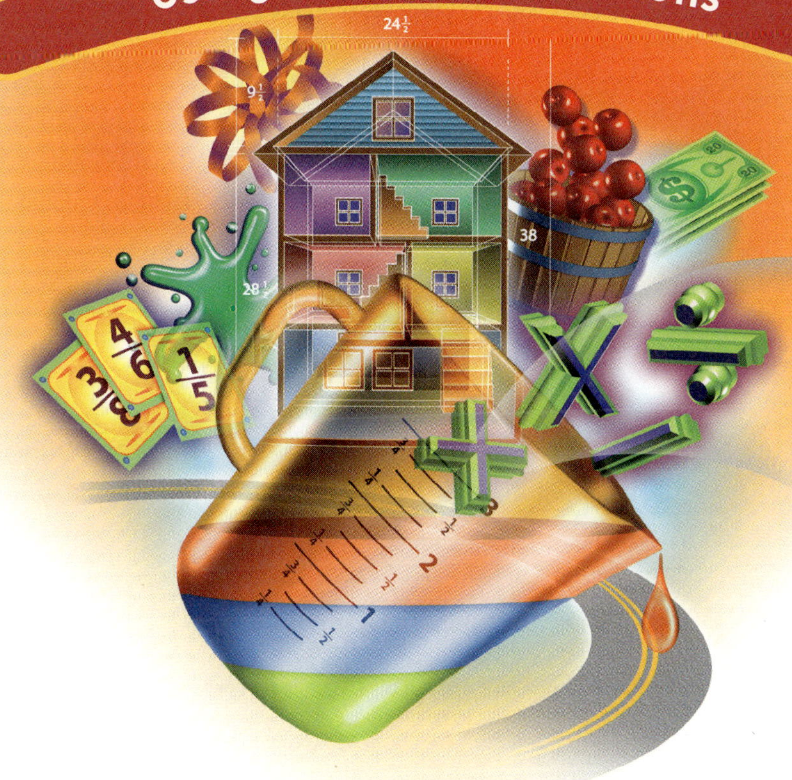

Glenda Lappan
James T. Fey
William M. Fitzgerald
Susan N. Friel
Elizabeth Difanis Phillips

Boston, Massachusetts · Glenview, Illinois · Shoreview, Minnesota · Upper Saddle River, New Jersey

Connected Mathematics™ was developed at Michigan State University with financial support from the Michigan State University Office of the Provost, Computing and Technology, and the College of Natural Science.

This material is based upon work supported by the National Science Foundation under Grant No. MDR 9150217 and Grant No. ESI 9986372. Opinions expressed are those of the authors and not necessarily those of the Foundation.

The Michigan State University authors and administration have agreed that all MSU royalties arising from this publication will be devoted to purposes supported by the MSU Mathematics Education Enrichment Fund.

Acknowledgments appear on page 73, which constitutes an extension of this copyright page.

13-digit ISBN 978-0-13-366132-3
10-digit ISBN 0-13-366132-6
2 3 4 5 6 7 8 9 10 11 10 09 08

Authors of Connected Mathematics

(from left to right) Glenda Lappan, Betty Phillips, Susan Friel, Bill Fitzgerald, Jim Fey

Glenda Lappan is a University Distinguished Professor in the Department of Mathematics at Michigan State University. Her research and development interests are in the connected areas of students' learning of mathematics and mathematics teachers' professional growth and change related to the development and enactment of K–12 curriculum materials.

James T. Fey is a Professor of Curriculum and Instruction and Mathematics at the University of Maryland. His consistent professional interest has been development and research focused on curriculum materials that engage middle and high school students in problem-based collaborative investigations of mathematical ideas and their applications.

William M. Fitzgerald (*Deceased*) was a Professor in the Department of Mathematics at Michigan State University. His early research was on the use of concrete materials in supporting student learning and led to the development of teaching materials for laboratory environments. Later he helped develop a teaching model to support student experimentation with mathematics.

Susan N. Friel is a Professor of Mathematics Education in the School of Education at the University of North Carolina at Chapel Hill. Her research interests focus on statistics education for middle-grade students and, more broadly, on teachers' professional development and growth in teaching mathematics K–8.

Elizabeth Difanis Phillips is a Senior Academic Specialist in the Mathematics Department of Michigan State University. She is interested in teaching and learning mathematics for both teachers and students. These interests have led to curriculum and professional development projects at the middle school and high school levels, as well as projects related to the teaching and learning of algebra across the grades.

CMP2 Development Staff

Teacher Collaborator in Residence

Yvonne Grant
Michigan State University

Administrative Assistant

Judith Martus Miller
Michigan State University

Production and Field Site Manager

Lisa Keller
Michigan State University

Technical and Editorial Support

Brin Keller, Peter Lappan, Jim Laser, Michael Masterson, Stacey Miceli

Assessment Team

June Bailey and **Debra Sobko** (Apollo Middle School, Rochester, New York), **George Bright** (University of North Carolina, Greensboro), **Gwen Ranzau Campbell** (Sunrise Park Middle School, White Bear Lake, Minnesota), **Holly DeRosia, Kathy Dole,** and **Teri Keusch** (Portland Middle School, Portland, Michigan), **Mary Beth Schmitt** (Traverse City East Junior High School, Traverse City, Michigan), **Genni Steele** (Central Middle School, White Bear Lake, Minnesota), **Jacqueline Stewart** (Okemos, Michigan), **Elizabeth Tye** (Magnolia Junior High School, Magnolia, Arkansas)

Development Assistants

At Lansing Community College *Undergraduate Assistant:* **James Brinegar**

At Michigan State University *Graduate Assistants:* **Dawn Berk, Emily Bouck, Bulent Buyukbozkirli, Kuo-Liang Chang, Christopher Danielson, Srinivasa Dharmavaram, Deb Johanning, Kelly Rivette, Sarah Sword, Tat Ming Sze, Marie Turini, Jeffrey Wanko;** *Undergraduate Assistants:* **Jeffrey Chapin, Jade Corsé, Elisha Hardy, Alisha Harold, Elizabeth Keusch, Julia Letoutchaia, Karen Loeffler, Brian Oliver, Carl Oliver, Evonne Pedawi, Lauren Rebrovich**

At the University of Maryland *Graduate Assistants:* **Kim Harris Bethea, Kara Karch**

At the University of North Carolina (Chapel Hill) *Graduate Assistants:* **Mark Ellis, Trista Stearns;** *Undergraduate Assistant:* **Daniel Smith**

Advisory Board for CMP2

Thomas Banchoff
Professor of Mathematics
Brown University
Providence, Rhode Island

Anne Bartel
Mathematics Coordinator
Minneapolis Public Schools
Minneapolis, Minnesota

Hyman Bass
Professor of Mathematics
University of Michigan
Ann Arbor, Michigan

Joan Ferrini-Mundy
Associate Dean of the College of Natural Science; Professor
Michigan State University
East Lansing, Michigan

James Hiebert
Professor
University of Delaware
Newark, Delaware

Susan Hudson Hull
Charles A. Dana Center
University of Texas
Austin, Texas

Michele Luke
Mathematics Curriculum Coordinator
West Junior High
Minnetonka, Minnesota

Kay McClain
Professor of Mathematics Education
Vanderbilt University
Nashville, Tennessee

Edward Silver
Professor; Chair of Educational Studies
University of Michigan
Ann Arbor, Michigan

Judith Sowder
Professor Emerita
San Diego State University
San Diego, California

Lisa Usher
Mathematics Resource Teacher
California Academy of Mathematics and Science
San Pedro, California

Field Test Sites for CMP2

During the development of the revised edition of *Connected Mathematics* (CMP2), more than 100 classroom teachers have field-tested materials at 49 school sites in 12 states and the District of Columbia. This classroom testing occurred over three academic years (2001 through 2004), allowing careful study of the effectiveness of each of the 24 units that comprise the program. A special thanks to the students and teachers at these pilot schools.

Arkansas

Magnolia Public Schools
Kittena Bell*, Judith Trowell*; *Central Elementary School:* Maxine Broom, Betty Eddy, Tiffany Fallin, Bonnie Flurry, Carolyn Monk, Elizabeth Tye; *Magnolia Junior High School:* Monique Bryan, Ginger Cook, David Graham, Shelby Lamkin

Colorado

Boulder Public Schools
Nevin Platt Middle School: Judith Koenig

St. Vrain Valley School District, Longmont
Westview Middle School: Colleen Beyer, Kitty Canupp, Ellie Decker*, Peggy McCarthy, Tanya deNobrega, Cindy Payne, Ericka Pilon, Andrew Roberts

District of Columbia

Capitol Hill Day School: Ann Lawrence

Georgia

University of Georgia, Athens
Brad Findell

Madison Public Schools
Morgan County Middle School: Renee Burgdorf, Lynn Harris, Nancy Kurtz, Carolyn Stewart

Maine

Falmouth Public Schools
Falmouth Middle School: Donna Erikson, Joyce Hebert, Paula Hodgkins, Rick Hogan, David Legere, Cynthia Martin, Barbara Stiles, Shawn Towle*

Michigan

Portland Public Schools
Portland Middle School: Mark Braun, Holly DeRosia, Kathy Dole*, Angie Foote, Teri Keusch, Tammi Wardwell

Traverse City Area Public Schools
Bertha Vos Elementary: Kristin Sak; *Central Grade School:* Michelle Clark; Jody Meyers; *Eastern Elementary:* Karrie Tufts; *Interlochen Elementary:* Mary McGee-Cullen; *Long Lake Elementary:* Julie Faulkner*, Charlie Maxbauer, Katherine Sleder; *Norris Elementary:* Hope Slanaker; *Oak Park Elementary:* Jessica Steed; *Traverse Heights Elementary:* Jennifer Wolfert; *Westwoods Elementary:* Nancy Conn; *Old Mission Peninsula School:* Deb Larimer; *Traverse City East Junior High:* Ivanka Berkshire, Ruthanne Kladder, Jan Palkowski, Jane Peterson, Mary Beth Schmitt; *Traverse City West Junior High:* Dan Fouch*, Ray Fouch

Sturgis Public Schools
Sturgis Middle School: Ellen Eisele

Minnesota

Burnsville School District 191
Hidden Valley Elementary: Stephanie Cin, Jane McDevitt

Hopkins School District 270
Alice Smith Elementary: Sandra Cowing, Kathleen Gustafson, Martha Mason, Scott Stillman; *Eisenhower Elementary:* Chad Bellig, Patrick Berger, Nancy Glades, Kye Johnson, Shane Wasserman, Victoria Wilson; *Gatewood Elementary:* Sarah Ham, Julie Kloos, Janine Pung, Larry Wade; *Glen Lake Elementary:* Jacqueline Cramer, Kathy Hering, Cecelia Morris, Robb Trenda; *Katherine Curren Elementary:* Diane Bancroft, Sue DeWit, John Wilson; *L. H. Tanglen Elementary:* Kevin Athmann, Lisa Becker, Mary LaBelle, Kathy Rezac, Roberta Severson; *Meadowbrook Elementary:* Jan Gauger, Hildy Shank, Jessica Zimmerman; *North Junior High:* Laurel Hahn, Kristin Lee, Jodi Markuson, Bruce Mestemacher, Laurel Miller, Bonnie Rinker, Jeannine Salzer, Sarah Shafer, Cam Stottler; *West Junior High:* Alicia Beebe, Kristie Earl, Nobu Fujii, Pam Georgetti, Susan Gilbert, Regina Nelson Johnson, Debra Lindstrom, Michele Luke*, Jon Sorenson

Minneapolis School District 1
Ann Sullivan K-8 School: Bronwyn Collins; Anne Bartel* (Curriculum and Instruction Office)

Wayzata School District 284
Central Middle School: Sarajane Myers, Dan Nielsen, Tanya Ravenholdt

White Bear Lake School District 624
Central Middle School: Amy Jorgenson, Michelle Reich, Brenda Sammon

New York

New York City Public Schools
IS 89: Yelena Aynbinder, Chi-Man Ng, Nina Rapaport, Joel Spengler, Phyllis Tam*, Brent Wyso; *Wagner Middle School:* Jason Appel, Intissar Fernandez, Yee Gee Get, Richard Goldstein, Irving Marcus, Sue Norton, Bernadita Owens, Jennifer Rehn*, Kevin Yuhas

---

* indicates a Field Test Site Coordinator

Ohio

Talawanda School District, Oxford
Talawanda Middle School: Teresa Abrams, Larry Brock, Heather Brosey, Julie Churchman, Monna Even, Karen Fitch, Bob George, Amanda Klee, Pat Meade, Sandy Montgomery, Barbara Sherman, Lauren Steidl

Miami University
Jeffrey Wanko*

Springfield Public Schools
Rockway School: Jim Mamer

Pennsylvania

Pittsburgh Public Schools
Kenneth Labuskes, Marianne O'Connor, Mary Lynn Raith*; *Arthur J. Rooney Middle School:* David Hairston, Stamatina Mousetis, Alfredo Zangaro; *Frick International Studies Academy:* Suzanne Berry, Janet Falkowski, Constance Finseth, Romika Hodge, Frank Machi; *Reizenstein Middle School:* Jeff Baldwin, James Brautigam, Lorena Burnett, Glen Cobbett, Michael Jordan, Margaret Lazur, Melissa Munnell, Holly Neely, Ingrid Reed, Dennis Reft

Texas

Austin Independent School District
Bedichek Middle School: Lisa Brown, Jennifer Glasscock, Vicki Massey

El Paso Independent School District
Cordova Middle School: Armando Aguirre, Anneliesa Durkes, Sylvia Guzman, Pat Holguin*, William Holguin, Nancy Nava, Laura Orozco, Michelle Peña, Roberta Rosen, Patsy Smith, Jeremy Wolf

Plano Independent School District
Patt Henry, James Wohlgehagen*; *Frankford Middle School:* Mandy Baker, Cheryl Butsch, Amy Dudley, Betsy Eshelman, Janet Greene, Cort Haynes, Kathy Letchworth, Kay Marshall, Kelly McCants, Amy Reck, Judy Scott, Syndy Snyder, Lisa Wang; *Wilson Middle School:* Darcie Bane, Amanda Bedenko, Whitney Evans, Tonelli Hatley, Sarah (Becky) Higgs, Kelly Johnston, Rebecca McElligott, Kay Neuse, Cheri Slocum, Kelli Straight

Washington

Evergreen School District
Shahala Middle School: Nicole Abrahamsen, Terry Coon*, Carey Doyle, Sheryl Drechsler, George Gemma, Gina Helland, Amy Hilario, Darla Lidyard, Sean McCarthy, Tilly Meyer, Willow Neuwelt, Todd Parsons, Brian Pederson, Stan Posey, Shawn Scott, Craig Sjoberg, Lynette Sundstrom, Charles Switzer, Luke Youngblood

Wisconsin

Beaver Dam Unified School District
Beaver Dam Middle School: Jim Braemer, Jeanne Frick, Jessica Greatens, Barbara Link, Dennis McCormick, Karen Michels, Nancy Nichols*, Nancy Palm, Shelly Stelsel, Susan Wiggins

Milwaukee Public Schools
Fritsche Middle School: Peggy Brokaw, Rosann Hollinger*, Dan Homontowski, David Larson, LaRon Ramsey, Judy Roschke*, Lora Ruedt, Dorothy Schuller, Sandra Wiesen, Aaron Womack, Jr.

---

* indicates a Field Test Site Coordinator

Reviews of CMP to Guide Development of CMP2

Before writing for CMP2 began or field tests were conducted, the first edition of *Connected Mathematics* was submitted to the mathematics faculties of school districts from many parts of the country and to 80 individual reviewers for extensive comments.

School District Survey Reviews of CMP

Madison School District #38 (Phoenix)

Arkansas
Cabot School District,
Little Rock School District,
Magnolia School District

California
Los Angeles Unified School District

Colorado
St. Vrain Valley School District (Longmont)

Florida
Leon County Schools (Tallahassee)

Illinois
School District #21 (Wheeling)

Indiana
Joseph L. Block Junior High (East Chicago)

Kentucky
Fayette County Public Schools (Lexington)

Maine
Selection of Schools

Massachusetts
Selection of Schools

Michigan
Sparta Area Schools

Minnesota
Hopkins School District

Texas
Austin Independent School District,
The El Paso Collaborative for Academic Excellence,
Plano Independent School District

Wisconsin
Platteville Middle School

Individual Reviewers of CMP

Arkansas
Deborah Cramer; Robby Frizzell *(Taylor)*; Lowell Lynde *(University of Arkansas, Monticello)*; Leigh Manzer *(Norfork)*; Lynne Roberts *(Emerson High School, Emerson)*; Tony Timms *(Cabot Public Schools)*; Judith Trowell *(Arkansas Department of Higher Education)*

California
José Alcantar *(Gilroy)*; Eugenie Belcher *(Gilroy)*; Marian Pasternack *(Lowman M. S. T. Center, North Hollywood)*; Susana Pezoa *(San Jose)*; Todd Rabusin *(Hollister)*; Margaret Siegfried *(Ocala Middle School, San Jose)*; Polly Underwood *(Ocala Middle School, San Jose)*

Colorado
Janeane Golliher *(St. Vrain Valley School District, Longmont)*; Judith Koenig *(Nevin Platt Middle School, Boulder)*

Florida
Paige Loggins *(Swift Creek Middle School, Tallahassee)*

Illinois
Jan Robinson *(School District #21, Wheeling)*

Indiana
Frances Jackson *(Joseph L. Block Junior High, East Chicago)*

Kentucky
Natalee Feese *(Fayette County Public Schools, Lexington)*

Maine
Betsy Berry *(Maine Math & Science Alliance, Augusta)*

Maryland
Joseph Gagnon *(University of Maryland, College Park)*; Paula Maccini *(University of Maryland, College Park)*

Massachusetts
George Cobb *(Mt. Holyoke College, South Hadley)*; Cliff Kanold *(University of Massachusetts, Amherst)*

Michigan
Mary Bouck *(Farwell Area Schools)*; Carol Dorer *(Slauson Middle School, Ann Arbor)*; Carrie Heaney *(Forsythe Middle School, Ann Arbor)*; Ellen Hopkins *(Clague Middle School, Ann Arbor)*; Teri Keusch *(Portland Middle School, Portland)*; Valerie Mills *(Oakland Schools, Waterford)*; Mary Beth Schmitt *(Traverse City East Junior High, Traverse City)*; Jack Smith *(Michigan State University, East Lansing)*; Rebecca Spencer *(Sparta Middle School, Sparta)*; Ann Marie Nicoll Turner *(Tappan Middle School, Ann Arbor)*; Scott Turner *(Scarlett Middle School, Ann Arbor)*

Minnesota
Margarita Alvarez *(Olson Middle School, Minneapolis)*; Jane Amundson *(Nicollet Junior High, Burnsville)*; Anne Bartel *(Minneapolis Public Schools)*; Gwen Ranzau Campbell *(Sunrise Park Middle School, White Bear Lake)*; Stephanie Cin *(Hidden Valley Elementary, Burnsville)*; Joan Garfield *(University of Minnesota, Minneapolis)*; Gretchen Hall *(Richfield Middle School, Richfield)*; Jennifer Larson *(Olson Middle School, Minneapolis)*; Michele Luke *(West Junior High, Minnetonka)*; Jeni Meyer *(Richfield Junior High, Richfield)*; Judy Pfingsten *(Inver Grove Heights Middle School, Inver Grove Heights)*; Sarah Shafer *(North Junior High, Minnetonka)*; Genni Steele *(Central Middle School, White Bear Lake)*; Victoria Wilson *(Eisenhower Elementary, Hopkins)*; Paul Zorn *(St. Olaf College, Northfield)*

New York
Debra Altenau-Bartolino *(Greenwich Village Middle School, New York)*; Doug Clements *(University of Buffalo)*; Francis Curcio *(New York University, New York)*; Christine Dorosh *(Clinton School for Writers, Brooklyn)*; Jennifer Rehn *(East Side Middle School, New York)*; Phyllis Tam *(IS 89 Lab School, New York)*; Marie Turini *(Louis Armstrong Middle School, New York)*; Lucy West *(Community School District 2, New York)*; Monica Witt *(Simon Baruch Intermediate School 104, New York)*

Pennsylvania
Robert Aglietti *(Pittsburgh)*; Sharon Mihalich *(Pittsburgh)*; Jennifer Plumb *(South Hills Middle School, Pittsburgh)*; Mary Lynn Raith *(Pittsburgh Public Schools)*

Texas
Michelle Bittick *(Austin Independent School District)*; Margaret Cregg *(Plano Independent School District)*; Sheila Cunningham *(Klein Independent School District)*; Judy Hill *(Austin Independent School District)*; Patricia Holguin *(El Paso Independent School District)*; Bonnie McNemar *(Arlington)*; Kay Neuse *(Plano Independent School District)*; Joyce Polanco *(Austin Independent School District)*; Marge Ramirez *(University of Texas at El Paso)*; Pat Rossman *(Baker Campus, Austin)*; Cindy Schimek *(Houston)*; Cynthia Schneider *(Charles A. Dana Center, University of Texas at Austin)*; Uri Treisman *(Charles A. Dana Center, University of Texas at Austin)*; Jacqueline Weilmuenster *(Grapevine-Colleyville Independent School District)*; LuAnn Weynand *(San Antonio)*; Carmen Whitman *(Austin Independent School District)*; James Wohlgehagen *(Plano Independent School District)*

Washington
Ramesh Gangolli *(University of Washington, Seattle)*

Wisconsin
Susan Lamon *(Marquette University, Hales Corner)*; Steve Reinhart *(retired, Chippewa Falls Middle School, Eau Claire)*

Table of Contents

Bits and Pieces II

Understanding Fraction Operations

Unit Opener 2

Mathematical Highlights 4

Investigation 1 Estimating With Fractions 5

1.1 Getting Close: Using Benchmarks 5

1.2 Estimating Sums 8

ACE Homework 10

Mathematical Reflections 15

Investigation 2 Adding and Subtracting Fractions 16

2.1 Land Sections: Writing Addition and Subtraction Sentences 17

2.2 Visiting the Spice Shop: Using Addition and Subtraction 19

2.3 Just the Facts: Fact Families 21

2.4 Designing Algorithms for Addition and Subtraction 22

ACE Homework 24

Mathematical Reflections 31

Investigation 3 **Multiplying With Fractions** 32

3.1 **How Much of the Pan Have We Sold?:** A Model for Multiplication . . 32
3.2 **Finding a Part of a Part:** Another Model for Multiplication 34
3.3 **Modeling More Multiplication Situations** 36
3.4 **Changing Forms:** Multiplication With Mixed Numbers. 37
3.5 **Writing a Multiplication Algorithm** 38
ACE Homework.. 40
Mathematical Reflections 47

Investigation 4 **Dividing With Fractions** 48

4.1 **Preparing Food:** Dividing a Whole Number by a Fraction 49
4.2 **Fundraising Continues:** Dividing a Fraction by a Whole Number. . . . 50
4.3 **Summer Work:** Dividing a Fraction by a Fraction 52
4.4 **Writing a Division Algorithm** 53
ACE Homework... 55
Mathematical Reflections 62

Looking Back and Looking Ahead 63
English/Spanish Glossary 66
Academic Vocabulary... 69
Index 71
Acknowledgments 73

Bits and Pieces II

Understanding Fraction Operations

Last season Farmer Sam picked $1\frac{3}{4}$ bushels of tomatoes from his kitchen garden and $14\frac{1}{3}$ bushels from his canning garden. About how many total bushels of tomatoes did he harvest?

Blaine plans to paint a highway stripe that is $\frac{9}{10}$ of a mile long. He is $\frac{2}{3}$ of the way done when he runs out of paint. How long is the stripe he painted?

There are 12 baby rabbits at the pet store. Gabriella has $5\frac{1}{4}$ ounces of parsley to feed the rabbits as treats. She wants to give each rabbit the same amount. How much parsley does each rabbit get?

In *Bits and Pieces I*, you learned what fractions, decimals, and percents mean. In *Bits and Pieces II*, you will investigate situations in which you need to add, subtract, multiply, or divide fractions, such as those described on the previous page. You will decide which operation makes sense in each situation.

Knowing strategies for working with all kinds of numbers is very important. If you take part in developing these strategies, they will make more sense to you, and you will be able to apply them to other situations. You may already know some shortcuts for working with fractions. You can get the most out of this unit by thinking about why those shortcuts, and the strategies you develop with your class, make sense. Remember, it is not enough to get an answer to a problem. The real power is your ability to talk about your ideas and strategies and use them in new situations.

Mathematical Highlights

Understanding Fraction Operations

In *Bits and Pieces II*, you will develop an understanding of and strategies for the four basic arithmetic operations with fractions.

You will learn how to

- Use benchmarks and other strategies to estimate the reasonableness of results of operations with fractions
- Develop ways to model sums, differences, products, and quotients, including the use of areas, fraction strips, and number lines
- Look for rules to generalize patterns in numbers
- Use your knowledge of fractions and equivalence of fractions to develop algorithms for adding, subtracting, multiplying and dividing fractions
- Recognize when addition, subtraction, multiplication, or division is the appropriate operation to solve a problem
- Write fact families to show the inverse relationship between addition and subtraction, and between multiplication and division
- Solve problems using operations on fractions

As you work on the problems in this unit, make it a habit to ask questions about situations that involve fraction operations.

What models or diagrams might be helpful in understanding the situation and the relationships among quantities?

What models or diagrams might help decide which operation is useful in solving a problem?

What is a reasonable estimate for the answer?

Investigation 1

Estimating With Fractions

Sometimes when you need to find an amount, you do not need an exact answer. In these situations, making a reasonable estimate of the answer is good enough. This investigation will help you develop strategies for estimating sums and differences. The sums and differences will involve fractions, as well as decimals.

1.1 Getting Close

Getting Close is a game that will sharpen your estimating skills. In *Bits and Pieces I*, you used *benchmarks* to estimate fractions and decimals. Look at this set of benchmarks.

$$0 \quad \frac{1}{4} \quad \frac{1}{2} \quad \frac{3}{4} \quad 1 \quad 1\frac{1}{4} \quad 1\frac{1}{2} \quad 1\frac{3}{4} \quad 2$$

Which benchmark is $\frac{3}{8}$ nearest? Three-eighths is less than $\frac{1}{2}$, because it is less than $\frac{4}{8}$. Three-eighths is greater than $\frac{1}{4}$, because it is greater than $\frac{2}{8}$. In fact, $\frac{3}{8}$ is exactly halfway between $\frac{1}{4}$ and $\frac{1}{2}$.

Which benchmark is 0.58 nearest? Since $\frac{1}{2}$ is equal to 0.50, 0.58 is greater than $\frac{1}{2}$. You also know that 0.58 is less than $\frac{3}{4}$ or 0.75. So 0.58 is between $\frac{1}{2}$ and $\frac{3}{4}$, but it is closer to $\frac{1}{2}$.

Getting Ready for Problem 1.1

How can you use benchmarks to help you estimate the sum of two fractions? Think about the example below.

$$\frac{1}{2} + \frac{5}{8}$$

- Is the sum between 0 and 1 or between 1 and 2?
- Is the sum closest to 0, to 1, or to 2?

When you play the Getting Close game, you will use benchmarks and other strategies to estimate the sum of two numbers.

Getting Close Rules

Two to four players can play Getting Close.

Materials

- Getting Close game cards (one set per group)
- A set of four number squares (0, 1, 2, and 3) for each player

Playing

1. All players hold their 0, 1, 2, and 3 number squares in their hand.
2. The cards are placed face-down in a pile in the center of the table.
3. One player turns over two game cards from the pile. Each player mentally estimates the sum of the numbers on the two game cards. Each player then selects from their set the number square (0, 1, 2, or 3) closest to their estimate and places it face-down on the table.
4. After each player has played a number square, the players turn their number squares over at the same time.
5. The player whose number square is closest to the actual sum gets the two game cards. If there is a tie, all players who tied get one game card. Players who have tied may take a game card from the deck if necessary.
6. Players take turns turning over the two game cards.
7. When all cards have been used, the player with the most cards wins.

You may find benchmarks, fraction strips, number lines, diagrams, or changing a fraction to a decimal helpful in making estimates. You may discover other ways of thinking that help as well.

Problem 1.1 Using Benchmarks

Play Getting Close several times. Keep a record of the estimation strategies you find useful.

A. **1.** Describe or illustrate one estimation strategy that you found useful in the game.

2. For which pairs was it easy and for which pairs was it hard to estimate the sum? Why?

B. Suppose you played Getting Close with only these game cards:

1. What is the greatest sum possible with any two of the game cards shown?

2. What is the least sum possible with any two of the game cards shown?

ACE **Homework starts on page 10.**

1.2 Estimating Sums

In this problem, you will see several situations that use fractions and involve estimating sums. There are times when you should overestimate what is needed to make sure you have enough. Other times, you want to underestimate to make sure you do not take or assume too much.

Problem 1.2 Estimating Sums

A. Elaine is making a model of a house that she designed. She wants to put wood molding around two rooms in the model. She measures and finds that she needs $3\frac{1}{4}$ feet of molding for one room and $2\frac{3}{8}$ feet of molding for the other room. She has $5\frac{1}{2}$ feet of molding.

1. Estimate whether she has enough molding.
2. Describe your strategy for estimating the answer.
3. Is your estimate an overestimate or an underestimate of the sum?

B. Elaine asks her granddaughter, Madison, to make curtains for the windows in the two model rooms. The pattern for the first room calls for a $\frac{7}{12}$-yard strip of material. The pattern for the second room calls for a $\frac{5}{8}$-yard strip.

1. Should Madison underestimate or overestimate the amount of material she needs? Why?
2. She writes the following computation: $\frac{7}{12} + \frac{5}{8} = \frac{12}{20}$. Use estimation to check whether her computation is reasonable. Explain your thinking.
3. Madison's friend, Jamar, says that he can write $\frac{7}{12} + \frac{5}{8}$ using the same denominator. He writes $\frac{14}{24} + \frac{15}{24}$ and says, "Now the answer is easy."
   a. What do you think Jamar will give as the sum? Does his thinking make sense?
   b. Is this an exact answer or an estimate?

C. Elaine makes the lace edging that is used to decorate the curtains in the model house. She needs 5 yards of lace for the curtains. She has these lengths of lace on hand:

$1\frac{1}{3}$ yards $2\frac{5}{6}$ yards $\frac{7}{8}$ yard $\frac{5}{12}$ yard

1. Should Elaine underestimate or overestimate the amount of lace she has? Why?
2. Use estimation to tell whether she has enough lace.
3. Find equivalent fractions with the same denominator to represent the lengths of lace. How does this help you find the actual length of all the lace?

D. Estimate these sums and describe your thinking.

1. $\frac{2}{3} + \frac{1}{5}$ 2. $2\frac{1}{3} + 3\frac{2}{3}$ 3. $\frac{3}{4} + \frac{4}{3}$

ACE **Homework starts on page 10.**

Applications Connections Extensions

ACE

Applications

For Exercises 1–9, determine whether the number is closest to 0, $\frac{1}{2}$, or 1. Explain your reasoning.

1. $\frac{10}{9}$ **2.** $\frac{9}{16}$ **3.** $\frac{2}{15}$

4. $\frac{500}{1000}$ **5.** $\frac{5}{6}$ **6.** $\frac{48}{100}$

7. 0.67 **8.** 0.26 **9.** 0.0009999

For Exercises 10–15, determine whether the sum of the two Getting Close game cards is closest to 0, 1, 2, or 3. Explain.

10. $\frac{7}{8}$ and $\frac{4}{9}$ **11.** $1\frac{4}{10}$ and 0.375 **12.** $\frac{2}{5}$ and $\frac{7}{10}$

13. $1\frac{3}{4}$ and $\frac{1}{8}$ **14.** $1\frac{1}{3}$ and 1.3 **15.** 0.25 and $\frac{1}{8}$

For Exercises 16–18, you are playing a game called Getting Even Closer. In this game, you have to estimate sums to the nearest $\frac{1}{2}$, or 0.5. Decide if the sum of the two game cards turned up is closest to 0, $\frac{1}{2}$, or 1. Explain.

16. $\frac{3}{5}$ and $\frac{1}{10}$ **17.** $\frac{1}{4}$ and $\frac{1}{10}$ **18.** $\frac{1}{9}$ and $\frac{1}{8}$

19. Four students were asked the following question: "Can you find two fractions with a sum greater than $\frac{3}{4}$?" Explain whether each student's answer below is correct.

a. $\frac{1}{8} + \frac{2}{4}$ **b.** $\frac{3}{6} + \frac{2}{4}$ **c.** $\frac{5}{12} + \frac{5}{6}$ **d.** $\frac{5}{10} + \frac{3}{8}$

For: Help with Exercise 19
Web Code: ame-4119

For Exercises 20–25, find two fractions with a sum that is between the two given numbers.

20. 0 and $\frac{1}{2}$ **21.** $\frac{1}{2}$ and 1 **22.** 1 and $1\frac{1}{2}$

23. $1\frac{1}{2}$ and 2 **24.** 2 and $2\frac{1}{2}$ **25.** $2\frac{1}{2}$ and 3

26. Many sewing patterns have a $\frac{5}{8}$-inch border for sewing the seam. Is a $\frac{5}{8}$-inch border closest to 0, $\frac{1}{2}$, or 1 inch? Explain.

27. Last season Farmer Sam picked $1\frac{3}{4}$ bushels of tomatoes from his kitchen garden and $14\frac{1}{3}$ bushels from his canning garden. About how many total bushels of tomatoes did he harvest?

28. Suppose you mix $\frac{5}{8}$ cup of wheat flour with $1\frac{3}{4}$ cups of white flour. Do you have enough for a recipe that calls for $2\frac{1}{2}$ cups of flour?

29. Soo needs 2 yards of molding to put around the bottom of a stand. He has two pieces of molding: one is $\frac{7}{8}$ yard long and the other is $\frac{8}{7}$ yard long. Estimate whether he has enough molding. Explain.

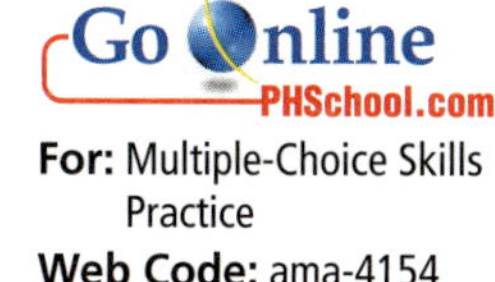

For: Multiple-Choice Skills Practice
Web Code: ama-4154

30. Julio is at the grocery store. He has \$10.00. Here is a list of the items he would like to buy. Use mental computation and estimation to answer parts (a)–(c).

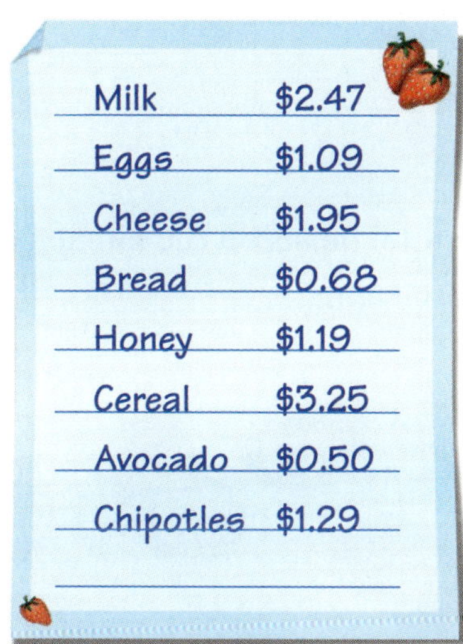

Item	Price
Milk	\$2.47
Eggs	\$1.09
Cheese	\$1.95
Bread	\$0.68
Honey	\$1.19
Cereal	\$3.25
Avocado	\$0.50
Chipotles	\$1.29

a. Can Julio buy all the items with the money he has? Explain.

b. If he has only \$5.00, what can he buy? Give two possibilities.

c. What different items can Julio buy to come as close as possible to spending \$5.00?

Connections

31. The rectangle shown represents $\frac{3}{4}$ of a whole.

a. Draw a rectangle representing the whole.

b. Draw a rectangle representing $\frac{5}{4}$ of the whole.

32. The rectangle shown represents 150% of a whole. Draw 100% of the same whole.

33. The beans shown represent $\frac{3}{5}$ of the total beans on the kitchen counter. How many total beans are there on the counter?

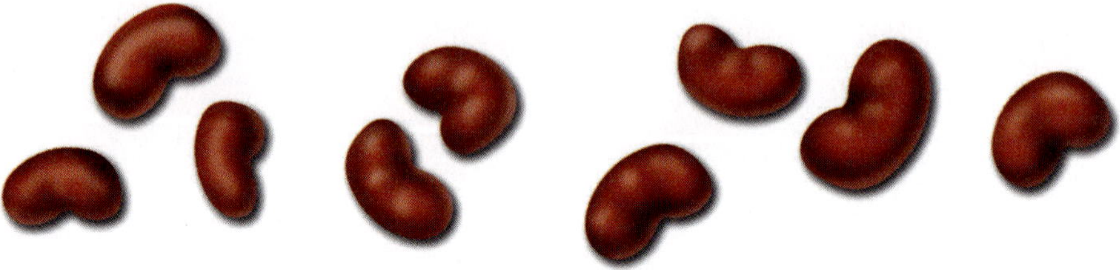

34. The following fractions occur so often in our lives that it is useful to quickly recall their decimal and percent equivalents.

$$\frac{1}{2} \quad \frac{1}{3} \quad \frac{1}{4} \quad \frac{2}{3} \quad \frac{3}{4} \quad \frac{1}{6} \quad \frac{1}{5} \quad \frac{1}{8}$$

a. For each of these important fractions, give the decimal and percent equivalents.

b. Draw a number line. On your number line, mark the point that corresponds to each fraction shown above. Label each point with its fraction, decimal, and percent equivalent.

35. **Multiple Choice** Choose the set of decimals that is ordered from least to greatest.

A. 5.603 5.63 5.096 5.67 5.599

B. 5.63 5.67 5.096 5.599 5.603

C. 5.096 5.63 5.67 5.603 5.599

D. 5.096 5.599 5.603 5.63 5.67

36. In which of the following groups of fractions can *all* the fractions be renamed as a whole number of hundredths? Explain your reasoning for each.

a. $\frac{3}{2}, \frac{3}{4}, \frac{3}{5}$

b. $\frac{7}{10}, \frac{7}{11}, \frac{7}{12}$

c. $\frac{2}{5}, \frac{2}{6}, \frac{2}{8}$

d. $\frac{11}{5}, \frac{11}{10}, \frac{11}{20}$

Connections

For Exercises 37–40, copy the figure onto your paper. Then, divide the figure into fourths. Shade $\frac{1}{4}$ of the figure.

37.

38.

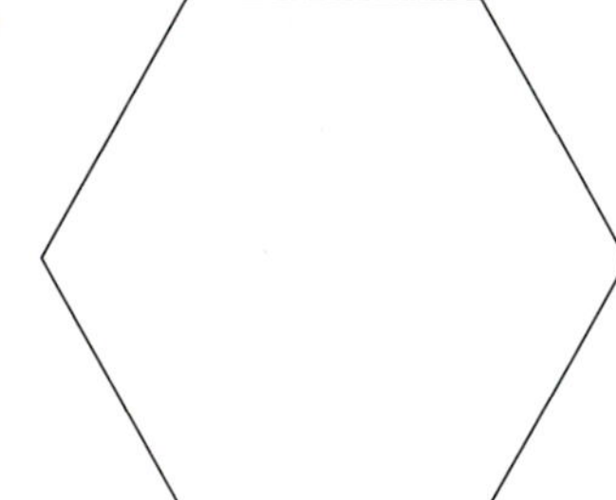

39.

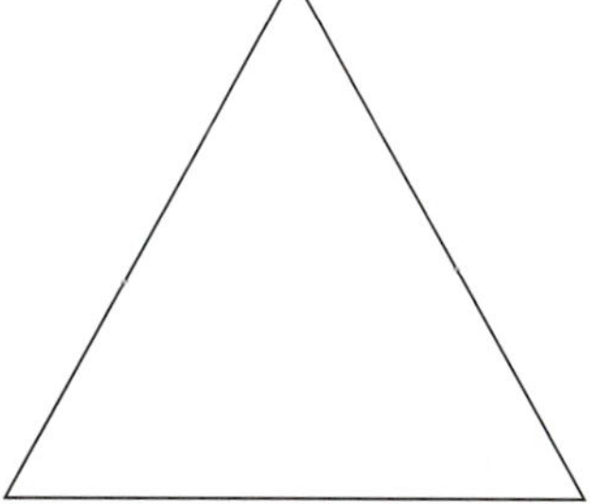

40.

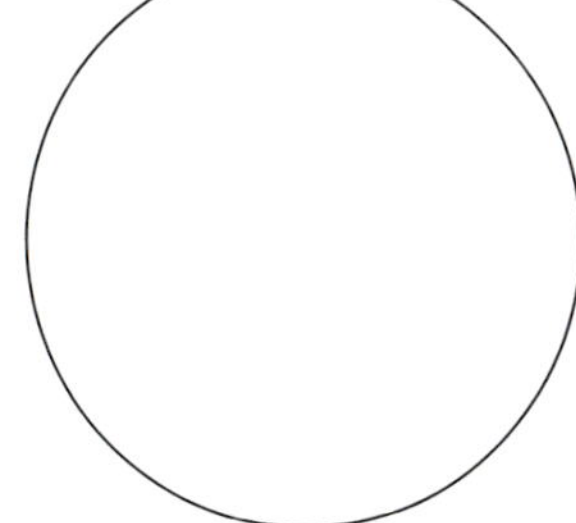

In Exercises 41 and 42, craft paint has spilled on the page, covering part of the fraction strips. Use what is showing to reason about each pair of strips. Find the equivalent fractions indicated by the question marks.

41.

?

?

42.

?

?

Extensions

For Exercises 43–46, name a fraction in the given interval.

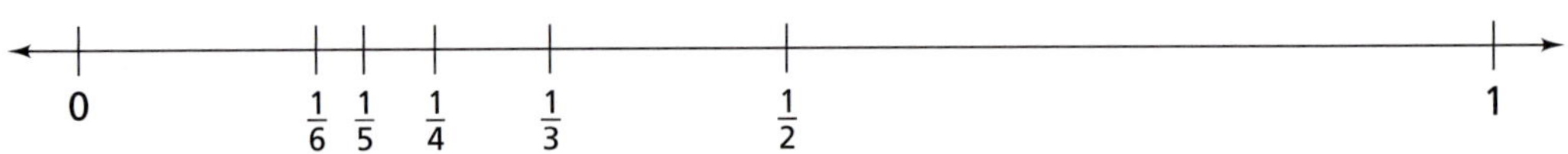

43. between $\frac{1}{3}$ and $\frac{1}{2}$

44. between $\frac{1}{4}$ and $\frac{1}{3}$

45. between $\frac{1}{5}$ and $\frac{1}{4}$

46. between $\frac{1}{6}$ and $\frac{1}{5}$

47. In Exercises 43–46, is it possible to find another fraction in each interval? Why or why not?

Mathematical Reflections 1

In this investigation, you developed strategies for estimating the sum of fractions and decimals. These questions will help you to summarize what you have learned.

Think about your answers to these questions. Discuss your ideas with other students and your teacher. Then write a summary of your findings in your notebook.

1. Describe at least two strategies for estimating fraction sums. Give an example for each strategy. Explain how each strategy is useful.
2. How do you decide whether an overestimate or an underestimate is most helpful? Give examples to help explain your thinking.

Investigation 2

Adding and Subtracting Fractions

Knowing how to combine and separate quantities is helpful in understanding the world around you. The mathematical names for combining and separating quantities are *adding* and *subtracting*.

For example, if you own two acres of land and you buy another half-acre lot, you will have $2 + \frac{1}{2}$, or $2\frac{1}{2}$, acres of land. The number sentence that shows this relationship is:

$$2 + \frac{1}{2} = 2\frac{1}{2}$$

The *sum* refers to the $2\frac{1}{2}$ acres of land you own.

If you then sell $\frac{3}{4}$ of an acre of your land, you will own $2\frac{1}{2} - \frac{3}{4}$ acres of land. The number sentence that shows this relationship is:

$$2\frac{1}{2} - \frac{3}{4} = 1\frac{3}{4}$$

The *difference* refers to the $1\frac{3}{4}$ acres of land you will own.

The problems in this investigation require you to add and subtract fractions. As you work, use what you have learned in earlier units and investigations about fractions and finding equivalent fractions. Practice writing number sentences to communicate your strategies for solving the problem.

2.1 Land Sections

When Tupelo Township was founded, the land was divided into sections that could be farmed. Each *section* is a square that is 1 mile long on each side. In other words, each section is 1 square mile of land. There are 640 acres of land in a square-mile section.

The diagram below shows two sections of land that are *adjacent*, or side by side. Each section is divided among several owners. The diagram shows the part of a section each person owns.

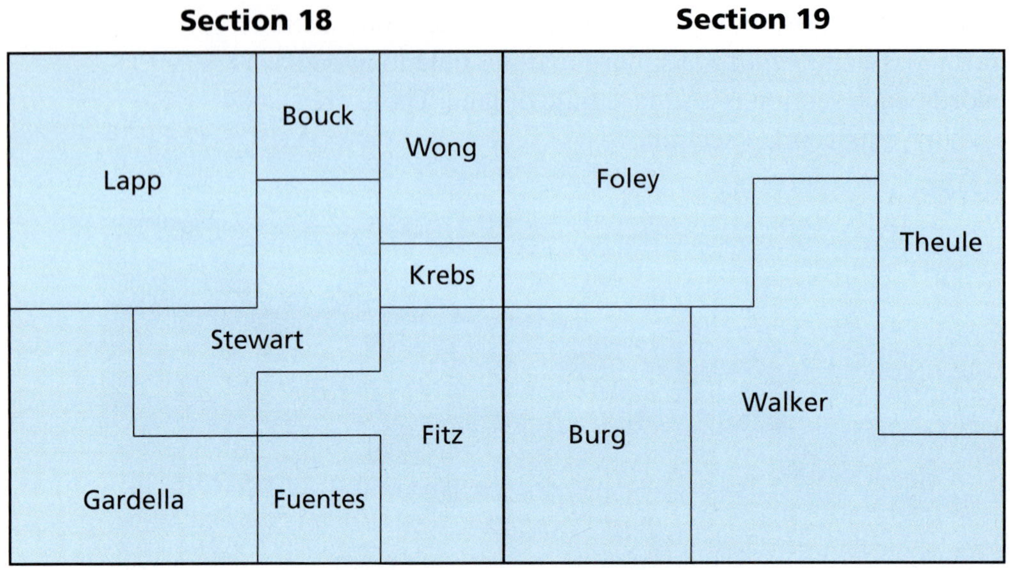

Section 18 **Section 19**

Bouck
Wong
Lapp
Foley
Theule
Krebs
Stewart
Walker
Fitz
Burg
Gardella
Fuentes

Problem 2.1 Writing Addition and Subtraction Sentences

A. What fraction of a section does each person own? Explain.

B. Suppose Fuentes buys Theule's land. What fraction of a section will Fuentes own? Write a number sentence to show your solution.

C. **1.** Find a group of owners whose combined land is equal to $1\frac{1}{2}$ sections of land. Write a number sentence to show your solution.

2. Find another group of owners whose combined land is equal to $1\frac{1}{2}$ sections of land.

D. **1.** Bouck and Lapp claim that when their land is combined, the total equals Foley's land. Write a number sentence to show whether this is true.

2. Find two other people whose combined land equals another person's land. Write a number sentence to show your answer.

3. Find three people whose combined land equals another person's land. Write a number sentence to show your answer.

E. How many acres of land does each person own? Explain your reasoning.

F. Lapp and Wong went on a land-buying spree and together bought all the lots of Section 18 that they did not already own. First, Lapp bought the land from Gardella, Fuentes, and Fitz. Then Wong bought the rest.

1. When the buying was completed, what fraction of Section 18 did Lapp own?
2. What fraction of Section 18 did Wong own?
3. Who owned more land? How much more land did he or she own?

ACE **Homework starts on page 24.**

2.2 Visiting the Spice Shop

All over the world cooks use spices to add flavor to foods. Because recipe ingredients are often measured using fractions, cooking can involve adding and subtracting fractional quantities.

Reyna owns a spice shop in Tupelo Township. Some of her recipes are shown below.

Problem 2.2 Using Addition and Subtraction

Use number sentences to show your thinking.

A. Latisha buys the spices to make one batch of Spice Parisienne.

  1. How many ounces of spice does Latisha buy?

  2. a. Suppose she already has the nutmeg at home. How many ounces of spice does she buy?

  b. Show a way to determine the answer using subtraction.

B. Ms. Garza buys spices to make one batch of Garam Masala.

  1. How many ounces of spice does Ms. Garza buy?

  2. a. Suppose she already has enough cinnamon and coriander at home. How many ounces of spice does she buy?

  b. Show a way to determine the answer using subtraction.

C. Betty buys spices for her famous fruitcake.

  1. How many ounces of spice does Betty buy?

  2. Betty makes the fruitcake but forgets the nutmeg! How many ounces of spice does she actually use?

3. Tevin is allergic to cinnamon. If Betty removes cinnamon from the recipe for him, how many ounces of spice does she buy?

D. Use what you have learned to find the value for N that makes each sentence correct.

1. $1\frac{2}{3} + 2\frac{7}{9} = N$
2. $\frac{2}{5} + \frac{1}{4} = N$
3. $2\frac{3}{4} - 1\frac{1}{3} = N$
4. $3\frac{1}{6} - 1\frac{3}{4} = N$
5. $N + \frac{3}{4} = 1\frac{1}{2}$
6. $2\frac{2}{3} - N = 1\frac{1}{4}$

E. Describe a good strategy for adding and subtracting mixed numbers.

ACE **Homework starts on page 24.**

2.3 Just the Facts

In Problem 2.2, you wrote an addition or subtraction sentence to show a calculation you did. For each addition sentence you write, there are three related number sentences that show the same information.

addition sentence:	$2 + 3 = 5$
related number sentences:	$3 + 2 = 5$
	$5 - 2 = 3$
	$5 - 3 = 2$

These four number sentences form a **fact family.**

You can also create fact families with fractions. For example, $\frac{3}{4} + \frac{1}{8} = \frac{7}{8}$ has these three related number sentences:

$$\frac{1}{8} + \frac{3}{4} = \frac{7}{8}$$
$$\frac{7}{8} - \frac{3}{4} = \frac{1}{8}$$
$$\frac{7}{8} - \frac{1}{8} = \frac{3}{4}$$

You can write this entire fact family using eighths by changing $\frac{3}{4}$ to $\frac{6}{8}$. It looks like this:

$$\frac{6}{8} + \frac{1}{8} = \frac{7}{8}$$
$$\frac{1}{8} + \frac{6}{8} = \frac{7}{8}$$
$$\frac{7}{8} - \frac{6}{8} = \frac{1}{8}$$
$$\frac{7}{8} - \frac{1}{8} = \frac{6}{8}$$

Problem 2.3 Fact Families

A. For each number sentence, write its complete fact family.

1. $\frac{2}{3} + \frac{5}{9} = \frac{11}{9}$

2. $\frac{5}{10} - \frac{2}{5} = \frac{1}{10}$

B. For each mathematical sentence, find the value of N. Then write each complete fact family.

1. $3\frac{3}{5} + 1\frac{2}{3} = N$

2. $3\frac{1}{6} - 1\frac{2}{3} = N$

3. $\frac{3}{4} + N = \frac{17}{12}$

4. $N - \frac{1}{2} = \frac{3}{8}$

C. After writing several fact families, Rochelle claims that subtraction undoes addition. Do you agree or disagree? Explain your reasoning.

D. In the mathematical sentence below, find values for M and N that make the sum exactly 3. Write your answer as a sum that equals 3.

$$\frac{5}{8} + \frac{1}{4} + \frac{2}{3} + M + N = 3$$

ACE **Homework starts on page 24.**

2.4 Designing Algorithms for Addition and Subtraction

To become skilled in solving problems that involve addition and subtraction of fractions, you need a plan for carrying out computations. In mathematics, a plan, or a series of steps, for doing a computation is called an **algorithm** (AL guh rith um). For an algorithm to be useful, each step should be clear and precise.

In this problem, you develop algorithms for adding and subtracting fractions. You may develop more than one for each computation. You should understand and feel comfortable with at least one algorithm for adding fractions and at least one algorithm for subtracting fractions.

Problem 2.4 Designing Algorithms for Addition and Subtraction

A. **1.** Find the sums in each group.

Group 1	Group 2	Group 3
$2\frac{2}{9} + \frac{4}{9}$	$\frac{4}{9} + \frac{1}{3}$	$\frac{1}{8} + \frac{2}{3}$
$\frac{5}{8} + \frac{1}{8}$	$2\frac{1}{2} + \frac{5}{12}$	$\frac{2}{9} + 3\frac{1}{4}$
$\frac{3}{5} + \frac{9}{5}$	$\frac{7}{8} + \frac{1}{2}$	$3\frac{4}{5} + 3\frac{3}{4}$

2. Describe what the problems in each group have in common.

3. Make up one new problem that fits in each group.

4. Write an algorithm that will work for adding *any* two fractions including mixed numbers. Test your algorithm on the problems in the table. If necessary, change your algorithm until you think it will work all the time.

B. **1.** Find the differences in each group.

Group 1	Group 2	Group 3
$3\frac{5}{6} - \frac{1}{6}$	$1\frac{3}{4} - \frac{1}{8}$	$3\frac{5}{6} - 1\frac{1}{4}$
$\frac{11}{7} - \frac{1}{7}$	$2\frac{7}{16} - 2\frac{1}{4}$	$\frac{1}{4} - \frac{1}{5}$
$1\frac{2}{3} - \frac{1}{3}$	$6\frac{7}{8} - 3\frac{3}{4}$	$4\frac{3}{5} - \frac{1}{3}$

2. Describe what the problems in each group have in common.

3. Make up one new problem that fits in each group.

4. Write an algorithm that will work for subtracting *any* two fractions, including mixed numbers. Test your algorithm on the problems in the table.

5. Describe how the subtraction problems below are different from the problems in the subtraction table in part (1).

Group 1	Group 2	Group 3
$1\frac{1}{3} - \frac{2}{3}$	$6\frac{3}{4} - 3\frac{7}{8}$	$3\frac{1}{4} - 1\frac{5}{6}$

6. If needed, change your algorithm until you think it will work all the time.

C. Use your algorithms for addition and subtraction to find each sum or difference.

1. $8 - 2\frac{2}{3}$ **2.** $8\frac{2}{3} - 2$ **3.** $2\frac{7}{16} + \frac{4}{9}$ **4.** $1\frac{4}{5} + 1\frac{5}{6} + 1\frac{3}{4}$

ACE Homework starts on page 24.

Applications Connections Extensions

Applications

1. The Langstons planted a big garden with flowers to sell to florists.

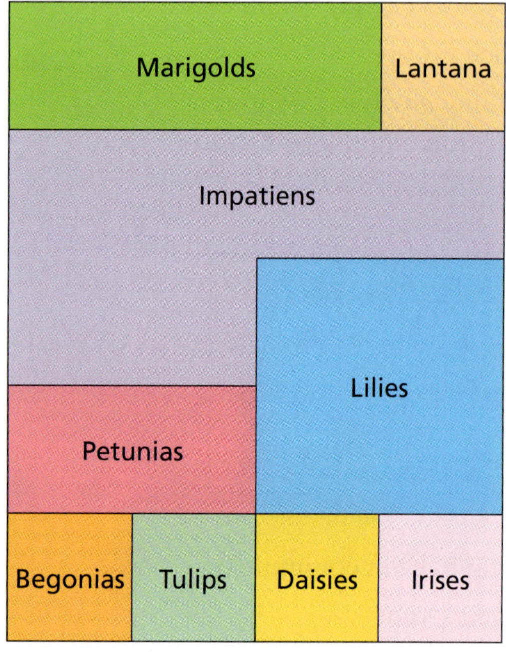

a. What fraction of the garden is planted with each type of flower?

b. How much more of the garden is planted with lilies than daisies?

c. Suppose the Langstons replace the daisies and irises with lilies. What fraction of the garden would be planted with lilies?

d. Use fractions to explain whether the following sentence is correct or incorrect.

The plots used for growing marigolds and petunias are equivalent to the plot used to grow impatiens.

e. Use fractions to explain whether the following sentence is correct or incorrect.

Marigolds − Begonias = Petunias + Tulips

f. Look at the original garden plan. Find three different combinations of plots that total the fraction of the garden planted with impatiens. Write a number sentence for each combination.

Applications

2. A local magazine sells space for ads. It charges advertisers according to the fraction of a page each ad fills.

a. Advertisers purchase $\frac{1}{8}$ and $\frac{1}{16}$ of a page. What fraction of the page is used for ads?

b. What fraction of the page remains for other uses? Explain.

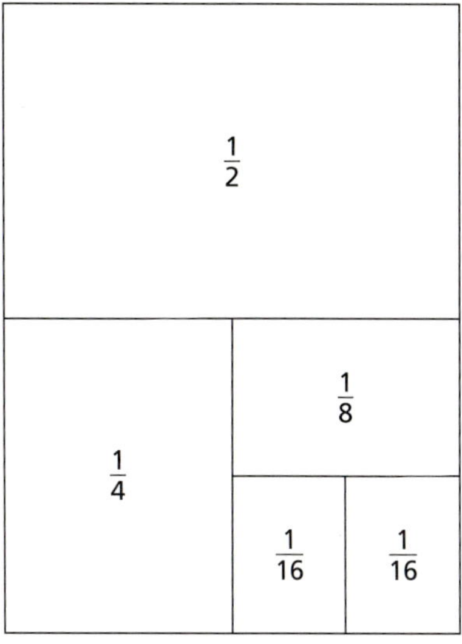

3. The Cool Sub Shop is having its grand opening. The owner buys three $\frac{1}{4}$-page ads, four $\frac{1}{8}$-page ads, and ten $\frac{1}{16}$-page ads. What is the total amount of ad space that the owner buys?

4. A local concert promoter purchases $2\frac{3}{4}$ pages of ads. When one of the concerts is cancelled, the promoter cancels $1\frac{5}{8}$ pages of ads. How much advertising space is the concert promoter actually using?

5. Rico and his friend eat part of a pan of lasagna. Rico eats $\frac{1}{16}$ of the lasagna, and his friend eats $\frac{1}{32}$ of the lasagna. How much of the lasagna is left?

6. Suppose you eat $\frac{3}{4}$ of a pizza and then eat $\frac{1}{8}$ of another pizza of the same size. How much of a whole pizza do you eat altogether?

For Exercises 7–12, find each sum or difference.

7. $8\frac{11}{12} - 2\frac{3}{4}$

8. $4\frac{4}{9} + 1\frac{2}{9}$

9. $2\frac{1}{8} + 3\frac{3}{4} + 1\frac{1}{2}$

10. $2\frac{7}{9} + 6\frac{1}{3}$

11. $11\frac{1}{2} - 2\frac{2}{3}$

12. $1\frac{2}{5} + 1\frac{1}{3}$

For: Multiple-Choice Skills Practice
Web Code: ama-4254

13. Find each sum. Describe any patterns that you see.

a. $\frac{1}{2} + \frac{1}{3}$

b. $\frac{2}{4} + \frac{2}{6}$

c. $\frac{6}{12} + \frac{4}{12}$

For Exercises 14–17, determine which sum or difference is greater. Show your work.

14. $\frac{2}{3} + \frac{5}{6}$ or $\frac{3}{4} + \frac{4}{5}$

15. $\frac{7}{6} - \frac{2}{3}$ or $\frac{3}{5} - \frac{5}{10}$

16. $\frac{1}{4} + \frac{5}{6}$ or $\frac{1}{5} + \frac{7}{8}$

17. $\frac{1}{16} + \frac{1}{12}$ or $\frac{5}{4} - \frac{4}{5}$

18. Write the complete fact family for $\frac{1}{16} + \frac{1}{12}$ and for $\frac{5}{4} - \frac{4}{5}$.

19. Find the value for N that makes each number sentence correct.

a. $\frac{2}{3} + \frac{3}{4} = N$ **b.** $\frac{3}{4} + N = \frac{4}{5}$ **c.** $N - \frac{3}{5} = \frac{1}{4}$

For Exercises 20–25, find each sum or difference.

20. $2\frac{5}{6} + 1\frac{1}{3}$ **21.** $15\frac{5}{8} + 10\frac{5}{6}$ **22.** $4\frac{4}{9} + 2\frac{1}{5}$

23. $6\frac{1}{4} - 2\frac{5}{6}$ **24.** $3\frac{1}{2} - 1\frac{4}{5}$ **25.** $4\frac{1}{3} - \frac{5}{12}$

26. Find each sum. Describe any patterns that you see.

a. $\frac{1}{2} + \frac{1}{4}$ **b.** $\frac{1}{3} + \frac{1}{6}$ **c.** $\frac{1}{4} + \frac{1}{8}$

d. $\frac{1}{5} + \frac{1}{10}$ **e.** $\frac{1}{6} + \frac{1}{12}$ **f.** $\frac{1}{7} + \frac{1}{14}$

27. Tony works at a pizza shop. He cuts two pizzas into eight equal sections each. Customers then eat $\frac{7}{8}$ of each pizza. Tony says that $\frac{7}{8} + \frac{7}{8} = \frac{14}{16}$, so $\frac{14}{16}$ of all the pizza was eaten. Is Tony's addition correct? Explain.

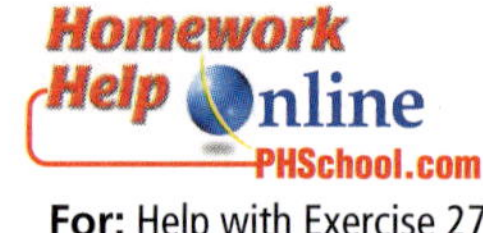

For: Help with Exercise 27
Web Code: ame-4227

Connections

28. Suppose you select a number in the interval from $\frac{1}{2}$ to $\frac{3}{4}$ and a number in the interval from $\frac{3}{4}$ to $1\frac{1}{4}$. What is the least their sum can be? What is the greatest their sum can be? Explain your reasoning. (Note: The numbers $\frac{1}{2}$ and $\frac{3}{4}$ are included in the interval from $\frac{1}{2}$ to $\frac{3}{4}$.)

29. One number is near the benchmark $\frac{1}{4}$, and another is near the benchmark $1\frac{1}{2}$. Estimate their sum. Explain.

For Exercises 30–35, find a value for N that will make the sentence true.

30. $\frac{3}{12} = \frac{N}{8}$ **31.** $\frac{N}{4} = \frac{6}{8}$ **32.** $\frac{1}{2} = \frac{N}{12}$

33. $\frac{N}{12} = \frac{2}{3}$ **34.** $\frac{N}{8} = \frac{14}{16}$ **35.** $\frac{5}{12} = \frac{10}{N}$

In Exercises 36–38, paint has spilled on the page, covering part of the fraction strips. Use what is showing to reason about each set of strips. Find the equivalent fractions indicated by the question marks.

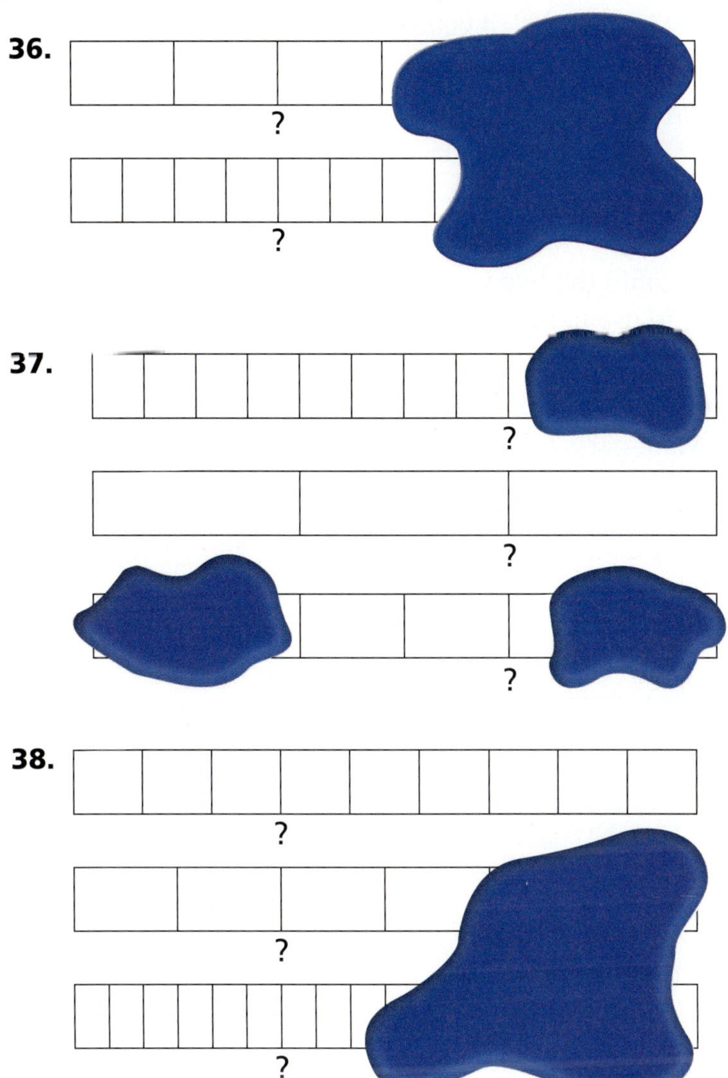

For Exercises 39 and 40, use the map of Tupelo Township from Problem 2.1.

39. **Multiple Choice** Choose the combination of landowners who together own exactly one hundred percent of a section.

A. Burg, Lapp, Wong, Fuentes, and Bouck

B. Burg, Lapp, Fuentes, Bouck, Wong, Theule, and Stewart

C. Lapp, Fitz, Foley, and Walker

D. Walker, Foley, Fitz, and Fuentes

40. Find two different combinations of landowners whose land is equal to 1.25 sections of land. Write number sentences to show your solutions.

Applications Connections

Copy each pair of numbers in Exercises 41–44. Insert <, >, or = to make a true statement.

41. 18.156 ■ 18.17

42. 3.184 ■ 31.84

43. 5.78329 ■ 5.78239

44. 4.0074 ■ 4.0008

45. When solving $\frac{7}{15} + \frac{2}{10}$, Maribel writes $\frac{70}{150} + \frac{30}{150}$.

a. Show why $\frac{70}{150} + \frac{30}{150}$ is equivalent to $\frac{7}{15} + \frac{2}{10}$.

b. Write two more addition problems that are equivalent to $\frac{7}{15} + \frac{2}{10}$.

c. Of the three problems, Maribel's and the two you wrote, which one do you think will be the easiest to use to find the sum? Why?

46. The model at the right represents $\frac{1}{3}$ of a whole. Use the model to name the amounts shown in parts (a) and (b).

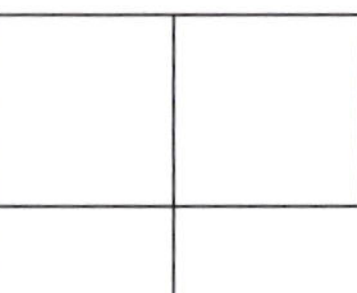

a.

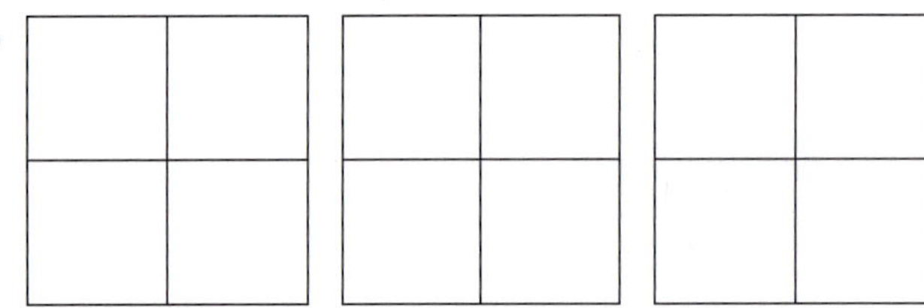

b.

47. The following model represents one whole.

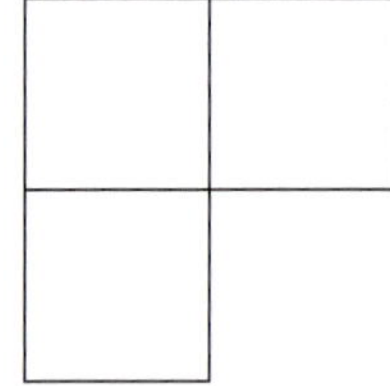

a. Draw a picture to represent $1\frac{1}{3} + \frac{1}{6}$.

b. Draw a picture to represent $2\frac{2}{3} - \frac{4}{3}$.

Extensions

48. *The Spartan* magazine wants to charge $160 for each full page of advertising.

a. Develop a pricing plan to show the cost for each size ad shown below. Explain.

$\frac{1}{32}$ page, $\frac{1}{16}$ page, $\frac{1}{8}$ page, $\frac{1}{4}$ page, $\frac{1}{2}$ page, 1 page

b. Use the pricing plan you developed. What is the bill for the Cool Sub Shop if the owner purchases three $\frac{1}{4}$-page ads, four $\frac{1}{8}$-page ads, and a $\frac{1}{16}$-page ad?

c. The senior class is raising money for their senior trip. They have $80 to spend on advertising. Geraldo says they can purchase two $\frac{1}{8}$-page ads and four $\frac{1}{16}$-page ads with their money. According to your pricing plan in part (a), is he correct? Explain.

d. Use your pricing plan from part (a). Find four different sets of ad sizes that the senior class can purchase for $80. Show why your answers are correct.

49. a. Find a number for each denominator to make the sentence true. If necessary, you may use a number more than once.

$$\frac{1}{\blacksquare} - \frac{1}{\blacksquare} = \frac{1}{\blacksquare}$$

b. Find another set of numbers that works.

50. It takes 8 people to clear an acre of weeds in 4 hours.

a. How many acres can 16 people clear in 4 hours?

b. How many acres can 2 people clear in 4 hours?

c. How many people are needed to clear 3 acres in 4 hours?

d. How many people are needed to clear 3 acres in 2 hours?

Connections Extensions

51. The sixth-grade students at Cleveland Middle School are selling popcorn as a fundraiser. They keep track of their progress using a number line like the one below:

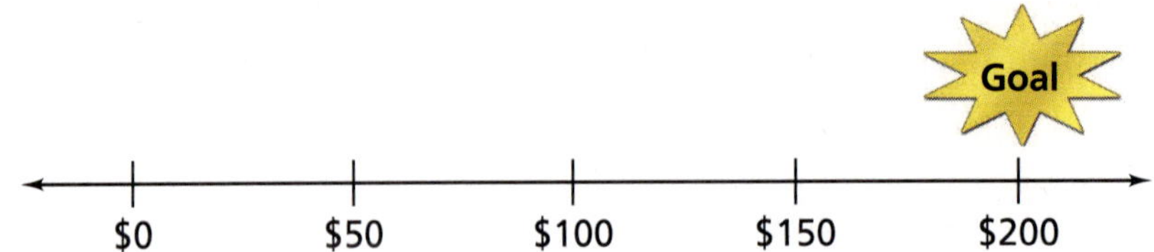

After Day 2, the students have not sold enough popcorn to make up for the money they spent getting started. Ms. Johnson suggests they change their number line to look like this:

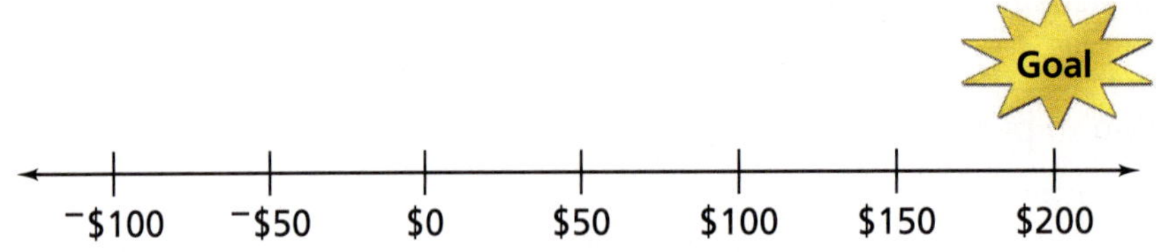

a. The students then plot this point to show their progress:

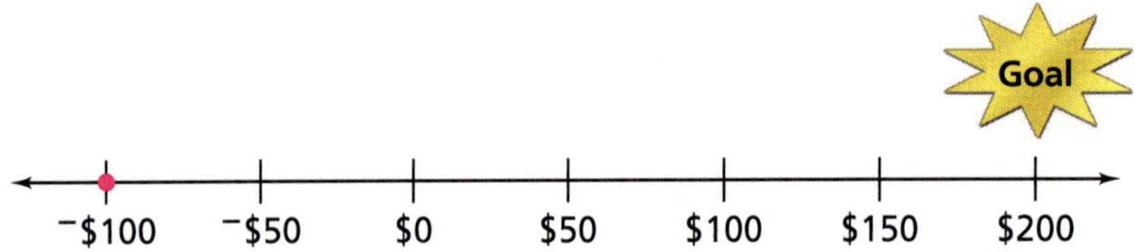

How much money have the sixth-graders lost?

b. After Day 4, the sixth-graders are doing better. They have lost a total of $25. Mark this point on a copy of the number line.

c. After Day 6, the sixth-graders are breaking even. This means they are no longer losing any money, but they are not gaining any money either. Mark their progress on your number line.

d. At the end of the fundraiser, the sixth-graders' number line looks like the one below. How much money have they raised?

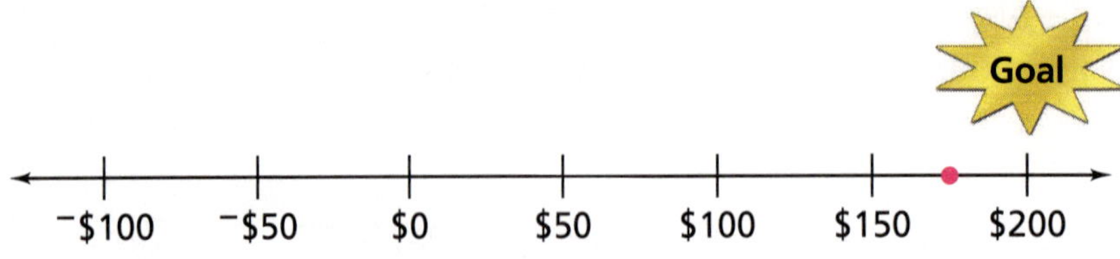

e. What fraction of their goal did they raise after they broke even?

Mathematical Reflections 2

In this investigation you explored ways to add and subtract fractions. These questions will help you to summarize what you have learned.

Think about your answers to these questions. Discuss your ideas with other students and your teacher. Then write a summary of your findings in your notebook.

1. Suppose you are helping a student who has not studied fractions. What is the most important thing you can say about adding or subtracting fractions?
2. Describe at least two things that you have to think about when you add or subtract with mixed numbers. Choose things that you do *not* need to think about when you add or subtract fractions.
3. Use an example to show how addition and subtraction of fractions are related in fact families.

Investigation 3

Multiplying With Fractions

Sometimes, instead of adding or subtracting fractions, you need to multiply them. For example, suppose you take inventory at the sporting goods store where you work. There are $13\frac{1}{2}$ boxes of footballs in the stock room, and there are 12 footballs in a full box. How can you find the total number of footballs without opening all the boxes? This situation requires multiplication.

In this investigation, you will relate what you already know about multiplication to situations involving fractions. Remember, to make sense of a situation you can draw a model or change a fraction to an equivalent form. You can also estimate to see if your answer makes sense.

3.1 How Much of the Pan Have We Sold?

Paulo and Shania work the brownie booth at the school fair. Sometimes, they have to find a fractional part of another fraction.

Problem 3.1 A Model for Multiplication

All the pans of brownies are square. A pan of brownies costs \$12. You can buy any fractional part of a pan of brownies and pay that fraction of \$12. For example, $\frac{1}{2}$ of a pan costs $\frac{1}{2}$ of \$12.

A. Mr. Williams asks to buy $\frac{1}{2}$ of a pan that is $\frac{2}{3}$ full.

1. Use a copy of the brownie pan model shown at the right. Draw a picture to show how the brownie pan might look before Mr. Williams buys his brownies.

Model of a Brownie Pan

2. Use a different colored pencil to show the part of the brownies that Mr. Williams buys. Note that Mr. Williams buys *a part of a part* of the brownie pan.

3. What fraction of a whole pan does Mr. Williams buy? What does he pay?

B. Aunt Serena buys $\frac{3}{4}$ of another pan that is half full.

1. Draw a picture to show how the brownie pan might look before Aunt Serena buys her brownies.

2. Use a different colored pencil to show the part of the brownies that Aunt Serena buys.

3. What fraction of a whole pan does Aunt Serena buy? How much did she pay?

C. When mathematicians write $\frac{1}{2}$ of $\frac{1}{4}$, they mean the operation of multiplication, or $\frac{1}{2} \times \frac{1}{4}$. When you multiply a fraction by a fraction, you are finding "a part of a part." Think of each example below as a brownie-pan problem in which you are buying part of a pan that is partly full—a part of a part.

1. $\frac{1}{3} \times \frac{1}{4}$ **2.** $\frac{1}{4} \times \frac{2}{3}$ **3.** $\frac{1}{3} \times \frac{3}{4}$ **4.** $\frac{3}{4} \times \frac{2}{5}$

D. Use estimation to decide if each product is greater than or less than 1. To help, use the "of" interpretation for multiplication. For example, in part (1), think "$\frac{5}{6}$ of $\frac{1}{2}$."

1. $\frac{5}{6} \times \frac{1}{2}$ **2.** $\frac{5}{6} \times 1$ **3.** $\frac{5}{6} \times 2$ **4.** $\frac{3}{7} \times 2$

5. $\frac{3}{4} \times \frac{3}{4}$ **6.** $\frac{1}{2} \times \frac{9}{3}$ **7.** $\frac{1}{2} \times \frac{10}{7}$ **8.** $\frac{9}{10} \times \frac{10}{7}$

ACE **Homework starts on page 40.**

3.2 Finding a Part of a Part

In *Bits and Pieces I*, you used thermometers to show what fraction of a fundraising goal had been met. These thermometers are like number lines. You mark thermometers in the same way you mark number lines to show parts of parts and to name the resulting piece. The fundraising thermometers can help you make sense of the number lines you will use in this problem.

One sixth-grade class raises $\frac{2}{3}$ of their goal in four days. They wonder what fraction of the goal they raise each day on average. To figure this out, they find $\frac{1}{4}$ of $\frac{2}{3}$. One student makes the drawings shown below:

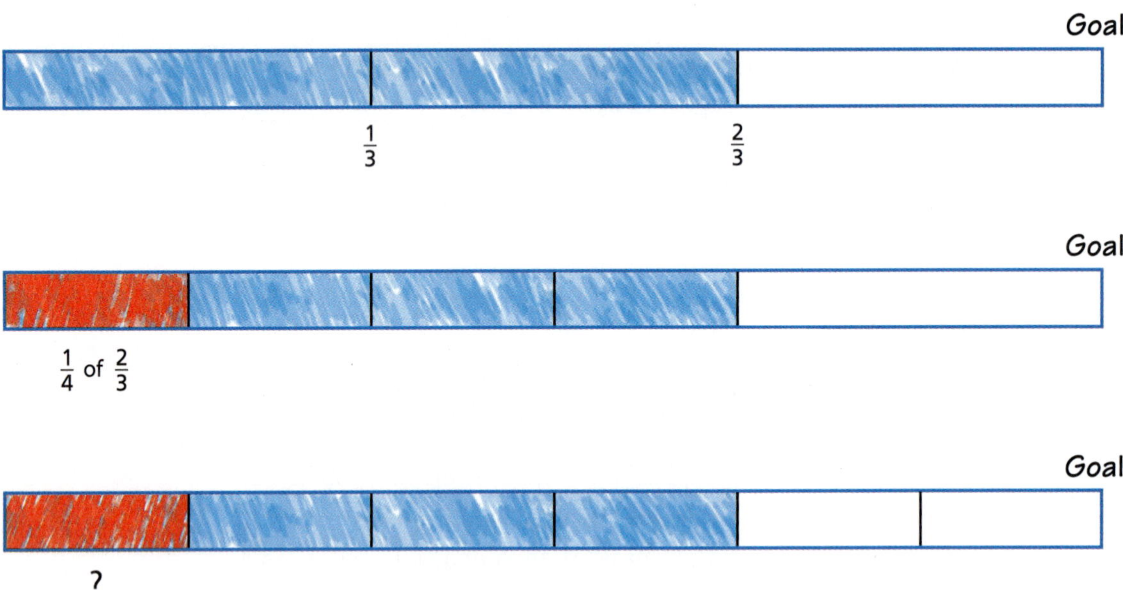

Getting Ready for Problem 3.2

The student above divides the fraction of the goal $\left(\frac{2}{3}\right)$ that is met in four days into fourths to find the length equal to $\frac{1}{4}$ of $\frac{2}{3}$. To figure out the new length, the student divides the whole thermometer into pieces of the same size.

What part of the whole thermometer is $\frac{1}{4}$ of $\frac{2}{3}$?

How would you represent $\frac{1}{4} \times \frac{2}{3}$ on a number line?

How would you represent $\frac{3}{4} \times \frac{2}{3}$ on a number line?

Problem 3.2 Another Model for Multiplication

A. 1. For parts (a)–(d), use estimation to decide if the product is greater than or less than $\frac{1}{2}$.

a. $\frac{1}{3} \times \frac{1}{2}$ **b.** $\frac{2}{3} \times \frac{1}{2}$ **c.** $\frac{1}{8} \times \frac{4}{5}$ **d.** $\frac{5}{6} \times \frac{3}{4}$

2. Solve parts (a)–(d) above. Use the brownie-pan model or the number-line model.

3. What patterns do you see in your work for parts (a)–(d)?

4. For part (b) above, do each of the following.

a. Write a word problem where it makes sense to use the brownie-pan model to solve the problem.

b. Write a word problem where it makes sense to use the number-line model to solve the problem.

B. Solve the following problems. Write a number sentence for each.

1. Seth runs $\frac{1}{4}$ of a $\frac{1}{2}$-mile relay race. How far does he run?

2. Mali owns $\frac{4}{5}$ of an acre of land. She uses $\frac{1}{3}$ of it for her dog kennel. How much of an acre is used for the kennel?

3. Blaine drives the machine that paints stripes along the highway. He plans to paint a stripe that is $\frac{9}{10}$ of a mile long. He is $\frac{2}{3}$ of the way done when he runs out of paint. How long is the stripe he painted?

C. What observations can you make from Questions A and B that help you write an algorithm for multiplying fractions?

D. Ian says, "When you multiply, the product is greater than each of the two numbers you are multiplying: $3 \times 5 = 15$, and 15 is greater than 3 and 5." Libby disagrees. She says, "When you multiply a fraction by a fraction, the product is less than each of the two fractions you multiplied." Who is correct and why?

ACE Homework starts on page 40.

3.3 Modeling More Multiplication Situations

In this problem, you will work with multiplication situations that use fractions, whole numbers, and mixed numbers. It is helpful to estimate first to see if your answer makes sense.

Getting Ready for Problem 3.3

Estimate each product to the nearest whole number (1, 2, 3, . . .).

$\frac{1}{2} \times 2\frac{9}{10}$ $\quad$ $1\frac{1}{2} \times 2\frac{9}{10}$ $\quad$ $2\frac{1}{2} \times \frac{4}{7}$ $\quad$ $3\frac{1}{4} \times 2\frac{11}{12}$

Will the actual product be greater than or less than your whole number estimate?

Problem 3.3 Modeling More Multiplication Situations

For each question:

- Estimate the answer.
- Create a model or a diagram to find the exact answer.
- Write a number sentence.

A. The sixth-graders have a fundraiser. They raise enough money to reach $\frac{7}{8}$ of their goal. Nikki raises $\frac{3}{4}$ of this money. What fraction of the goal does Nikki raise?

B. A recipe calls for $\frac{2}{3}$ of a 16-ounce bag of chocolate chips. How many ounces are needed?

C. Mr. Flansburgh buys a $2\frac{1}{2}$-pound wheel of cheese. His family eats $\frac{1}{3}$ of the wheel. How much cheese have they eaten?

D. Peter and Erin run the corn harvester for Mr. McGreggor. They harvest about $2\frac{1}{3}$ acres each day. They have only $10\frac{1}{2}$ days to harvest the corn. How many acres of corn can they harvest for Mr. McGreggor?

ACE Homework starts on page 40.

3.4 Changing Forms

You have developed some strategies for modeling multiplication and finding products involving fractions. This problem will give you a chance to further develop your strategies. Before you begin a problem, you should always ask yourself: "About how large will the product be?"

Getting Ready for Problem 3.4

Yuri and Paula are trying to find the following product.

$$2\frac{2}{3} \times \frac{1}{4}$$

Yuri says that if he rewrites $2\frac{2}{3}$, he can use what he knows about multiplying fractions. He writes:

$$\frac{8}{3} \times \frac{1}{4}$$

Paula asks, "Can you do that? Are those two problems the same?"

What do you think about Yuri's idea? Are the two multiplication problems equivalent?

Problem 3.4 Multiplication With Mixed Numbers

A. Use what you know about equivalence and multiplying fractions to first estimate, and then determine, the following products.

1. $2\frac{1}{2} \times 1\frac{1}{6}$
2. $3\frac{4}{5} \times \frac{1}{4}$
3. $\frac{3}{4} \times 16$
4. $\frac{5}{3} \times 2$
5. $1\frac{1}{3} \times 3\frac{6}{7}$
6. $\frac{1}{4} \times \frac{9}{4}$

B. Choose two problems from Question A. Draw a picture to prove that your calculations make sense.

C. Takoda answers Question A part (1) by doing the following:

$$\left(2 \times 1\frac{1}{6}\right) + \left(\frac{1}{2} \times 1\frac{1}{6}\right)$$

1. Do you think Takoda's strategy works? Explain.
2. Try Takoda's strategy on parts (2) and (5) in Question A. Does his strategy work? Why or why not?

D. For parts (1)–(3), find a value for N so that the product of $1\frac{1}{2} \times N$ is:

1. between 0 and $1\frac{1}{2}$
2. $1\frac{1}{2}$
3. between $1\frac{1}{2}$ and 2
4. Describe when a product will be less than each of the two factors.
5. Describe when a product will be greater than each of the two factors.

ACE **Homework starts on page 40.**

3.5 Writing a Multiplication Algorithm

Recall that an algorithm is a reliable mathematical procedure. You have developed algorithms for adding and subtracting fractions. Now you will develop an algorithm for multiplying fractions.

Problem 3.5 Writing a Multiplication Algorithm

A. 1. Find the products in each group below.

Group 1	Group 2	Group 3
$\frac{1}{3} \times \frac{3}{4}$	$2 \times 1\frac{7}{8}$	$3\frac{2}{3} \times 1\frac{1}{2}$
$\frac{1}{4} \times \frac{2}{5}$	$\frac{2}{5} \times 12$	$2\frac{1}{4} \times 2\frac{5}{6}$
$\frac{2}{3} \times \frac{5}{7}$	$6 \times 1\frac{3}{8}$	$1\frac{1}{5} \times 2\frac{2}{3}$

2. Describe what the problems in each group have in common.

3. Make up one new problem that fits in each group.

4. Write an algorithm that will work for multiplying *any* two fractions, including mixed numbers. Test your algorithm on the problems in the table. If necessary, change your algorithm until you think it will work all the time.

B. Use your algorithm to multiply.

1. $\frac{5}{6} \times \frac{3}{4}$ **2.** $1\frac{2}{3} \times 12$ **3.** $\frac{14}{3} \times \frac{10}{3}$ **4.** $\frac{2}{5} \times 1\frac{1}{2}$

C. Find each product. What pattern do you see? Give another example that fits your pattern.

1. $\frac{7}{8} \times \frac{8}{7}$ **2.** $\frac{1}{9} \times \frac{9}{1}$ **3.** $1\frac{2}{3} \times \frac{3}{5}$ **4.** $11 \times \frac{1}{11}$

ACE **Homework starts on page 40.**

Did You Know?

When you reverse the placement of the numbers in the numerator and the denominator, a new fraction is formed. This new fraction is the **reciprocal** of the original. For example, $\frac{7}{8}$ is the reciprocal of $\frac{8}{7}$, and $\frac{12}{17}$ is the reciprocal of $\frac{17}{12}$, or $1\frac{5}{12}$. Notice that the product of a fraction and its reciprocal is 1.

Applications

Connections

Extensions

Applications

1. Greg buys $\frac{2}{5}$ of a square pan of brownies that has only $\frac{7}{10}$ of the pan left.

a. Draw a picture of how the brownie pan might look before and after Greg buys his brownies.

b. What fraction of a whole pan does Greg buy?

2. Ms. Guerdin owns $\frac{4}{5}$ acre of land in Tupelo Township. She wants to sell $\frac{2}{3}$ of her land to her neighbor.

a. What fraction of an acre does she want to sell? Draw pictures to illustrate your thinking.

b. Write a number sentence that can be used to solve the problem.

3. Find each answer and explain how you know.

a. Is $\frac{3}{4} \times 1$ greater than or less than 1?

b. Is $\frac{3}{4} \times \frac{2}{3}$ greater than or less than 1?

c. Is $\frac{3}{4} \times \frac{2}{3}$ greater than or less than $\frac{2}{3}$?

d. Is $\frac{3}{4} \times \frac{2}{3}$ greater than or less than $\frac{3}{4}$?

4. a. Use a brownie-pan model to show whether finding $\frac{2}{3}$ of $\frac{3}{4}$ of a pan of brownies means the same thing as finding $\frac{3}{4}$ of $\frac{2}{3}$ of a pan of brownies.

b. If the brownie pans are the same size, how do the final amounts of brownies compare in the situations in part (a)?

c. What does this say about $\frac{2}{3} \times \frac{3}{4}$ and $\frac{3}{4} \times \frac{2}{3}$?

5. Find each product. Describe any patterns that you see.

a. $\frac{1}{2}$ of $\frac{1}{3}$ **b.** $\frac{1}{2}$ of $\frac{1}{4}$ **c.** $\frac{1}{2}$ of $\frac{2}{3}$ **d.** $\frac{1}{2}$ of $\frac{3}{4}$

Applications

6. Mrs. Mace's class is planning a field trip, and $\frac{3}{5}$ of her students want to go to Chicago. Of those who want to go to Chicago, $\frac{2}{3}$ say they want to go to Navy Pier. What fraction of the class wants to go to Navy Pier?

7. Min Ji uses balsa wood to build airplane models. After completing a model, she has a strip of balsa wood measuring $\frac{7}{8}$ yard left over. Shawn wants to buy half of the strip from Min Ji. How long is the strip of wood Shawn wants to buy?

8. Aran has a fruit roll-up for a snack. He gives half of it to Jon. Jon then gives Kiona $\frac{1}{3}$ of his part. How much of the fruit roll-up does each person get?

9. In Vashon's class, three fourths of the students are girls. Four fifths of the girls in Vashon's class have brown hair.
   a. What fraction represents the girls in Vashon's class with brown hair?
   b. How many students do you think are in Vashon's class?

10. Find each product.
   a. $\frac{1}{3}$ of $\frac{2}{3}$ b. $\frac{5}{6}$ of 3 c. $\frac{2}{3}$ of $\frac{5}{6}$ d. $\frac{2}{5}$ of $\frac{5}{8}$

11. Estimate each product. Explain.
   a. $\frac{2}{3} \times 4$ b. $2 \times \frac{2}{3}$ c. $2\frac{1}{2} \times \frac{2}{3}$

12. Esteban is making turtle brownies. The recipe calls for $\frac{3}{4}$ bag of caramel squares. The bag has 24 caramel squares in it.

   a. How many caramel squares should Esteban use to make one batch of turtle brownies?

   b. Esteban decides to make two batches of turtle brownies. Write a number sentence to show how many bags of caramel squares he will use.

13. Isabel is adding a sun porch onto her house. She measures and finds that covering the entire floor requires 12 rows with $11\frac{1}{3}$ tiles in each row. Write a number sentence to show how many tiles Isabel will use to cover the floor.

14. Judi is making a frame for her little sister's drawing. The wood strip for the frame is 1 inch wide. She allows two extra inches of wood for each corner. If the square is $11\frac{3}{8}$ inches on a side, how much wood should Judi buy?

15. Find each product. Look for patterns to help you.

   a. $\frac{1}{3} \times 18$ b. $\frac{2}{3} \times 18$ c. $\frac{5}{3} \times 18$ d. $1\frac{2}{3} \times 18$

16. Write a number sentence for each situation. (Assume that the fractions are all less than 1.)

   a. a fraction and a whole number with a whole number product

   b. a fraction and a whole number with a product less than 1

   c. a fraction and a whole number with a product greater than 1

   d. a fraction and a whole number with a product between $\frac{1}{2}$ and 1

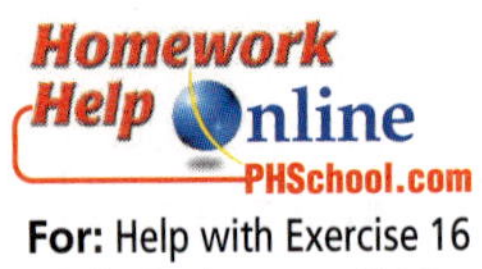

For: Help with Exercise 16
Web Code: ame-4316

Applications

17. Bonnie and Steve are making snack bags for their daughter's field hockey team. They put $\frac{3}{4}$ cup of pretzels, $\frac{2}{3}$ cup of popcorn, $\frac{1}{3}$ cup of peanuts, and $\frac{1}{4}$ cup of chocolate chips in each bag.

    a. If they want to make 12 bags, how much of each ingredient do they need?

    b. Bonnie decides that she would like to make snack bags for her card club. There are 15 people in the card club. How much of each ingredient will she need?

18. a. When Sierra gets home from school, $\frac{3}{4}$ of a sandwich is left in the refrigerator. She cuts the part remaining into three equal parts and eats two of them. What fraction of the whole sandwich did she eat?

    b. Write a number sentence to show your computation.

19. Mr. Jablonski's class is making fudge for a bake sale. He has a recipe that makes $\frac{3}{4}$ pound of fudge. There are 21 students in the class and each one makes one batch of fudge for the bake sale. How many pounds of fudge do the students make?

20. Carolyn is making cookies. The recipe calls for $1\frac{3}{4}$ cups of brown sugar. If she makes $2\frac{1}{2}$ batches of cookies, how much brown sugar will she need?

For Exercises 21–29, use your algorithm for multiplying fractions to determine each product.

21. $\frac{5}{12} \times 1\frac{1}{3}$	**22.** $\frac{2}{7} \times \frac{7}{8}$	**23.** $3\frac{2}{9} \times \frac{7}{3}$
24. $2\frac{2}{5} \times 1\frac{1}{15}$	**25.** $10\frac{3}{4} \times 2\frac{2}{3}$	**26.** $1\frac{1}{8} \times \frac{4}{7}$
27. $\frac{11}{6} \times \frac{9}{10}$	**28.** $\frac{9}{4} \times 1\frac{1}{6}$	**29.** $\frac{5}{2} \times \frac{8}{11}$

For: Multiple-Choice Skills Practice
Web Code: ama-4354

30. Multiple Choice Choose the number that, when multiplied by $\frac{4}{7}$, will be greater than $\frac{4}{7}$.

A. $\frac{1}{7}$ **B.** $\frac{7}{7}$ **C.** $\frac{17}{7}$ **D.** $\frac{4}{7}$

31. Multiple Choice Choose the number that, when multiplied by $\frac{4}{7}$, will be less than $\frac{4}{7}$.

F. $\frac{1}{7}$ **G.** $\frac{7}{7}$ **H.** $\frac{17}{7}$ **J.** $\frac{8}{7}$

32. Multiple Choice Choose the number that, when multiplied by $\frac{4}{7}$, will be exactly $\frac{4}{7}$.

A. $\frac{1}{7}$ **B.** $\frac{7}{7}$ **C.** $\frac{17}{7}$ **D.** $\frac{4}{7}$

33. **a.** How many minutes are in 1 hour?

b. How many minutes are in $\frac{1}{2}$ hour?

c. How many minutes are in 0.5 hour?

d. How many minutes are in 0.1 hour?

e. How many minutes are in 1.25 hours?

f. How many hours are in 186 minutes? Express this as a mixed number and as a decimal.

34. A magazine advertises stained glass sun catchers. The ad says that the actual sun catcher is $1\frac{3}{4}$ times the size shown in the picture. Mrs. Inman wants to know how tall the actual sun catcher is. She gets a ruler and measures the sun catcher in the picture. If the sun catcher in the picture is $1\frac{3}{8}$ inches high, how tall is the actual sun catcher?

35. Violeta and Mandy are making beaded necklaces. They have several beads in various colors and widths. As they design patterns to use, they want to figure out how long the final necklace will be. Violeta and Mandy have the following bead widths to work with.

Widths of Beads

Bead	Width
Trade Neck	$\frac{1}{4}$ inch
Medium Rosebud	$\frac{3}{8}$ inch
Large Rosebud	$\frac{7}{16}$ inch

a. If Mandy uses 30 Trade Neck beads, 6 medium Rosebud beads, and 1 large Rosebud bead, how long will her necklace be?

b. Violeta would like to make a 16-inch necklace by alternating medium and large Rosebud beads. She only has 8 medium Rosebud beads. If she uses 8 medium Rosebud beads and 8 large Rosebud beads, will her necklace be 16 inches long?

Connections

36. Here is a multiplication-division fact family:

$4 \times 5 = 20$ $\quad$ $5 \times 4 = 20$ $\quad$ $20 \div 4 = 5$ $\quad$ $20 \div 5 = 4$

For each number sentence, write a multiplication-division fact family.

a. $3 \times 6 = 18$ $\quad$ **b.** $16 \times 3 = 48$ $\quad$ **c.** $1\frac{1}{2} \times 7 = 10\frac{1}{2}$

d. $15 \div 3 = 5$ $\quad$ **e.** $100 \div 20 = 5$ $\quad$ **f.** $15 \div 1\frac{1}{2} = 10$

37. Roshaun and Lea go to an amusement park. Lea spends $\frac{1}{2}$ of her money, and Roshaun spends $\frac{1}{4}$ of his money. Is it possible for Roshaun to have spent more money than Lea? Explain your reasoning.

38. Bianca and Yoko work together to mow the lawn. Suppose Yoko mows $\frac{5}{12}$ of the lawn and Bianca mows $\frac{2}{5}$ of the lawn. How much lawn still needs to be mowed?

39. Joe and Ashanti need $2\frac{2}{5}$ bushels of apples to make applesauce. Suppose Joe picks $1\frac{5}{6}$ bushels of apples. How many more bushels need to be picked?

For Exercises 40–45, calculate each sum or difference.

40. $2\frac{2}{3} + 3\frac{5}{6}$

41. $2\frac{8}{10} + 2\frac{4}{5} + 1\frac{1}{2}$

42. $4\frac{3}{10} + 2\frac{2}{6}$

43. $5\frac{5}{8} - 2\frac{2}{3}$

44. $6\frac{7}{10} - 3\frac{4}{5}$

45. $8 - 3\frac{14}{15}$

46. Three students multiply $6 \times \frac{1}{5}$. Their answers are $\frac{6}{5}$, 1.2, and $1\frac{1}{5}$. Match each answer to the strategy described below that is most likely to produce it. Explain.

a. Fala draws six shapes, each representing $\frac{1}{5}$, and fits them together.

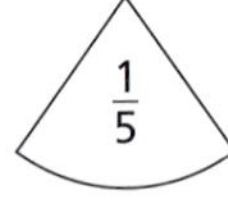

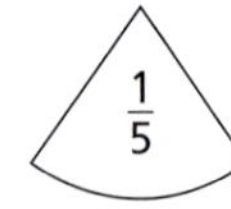

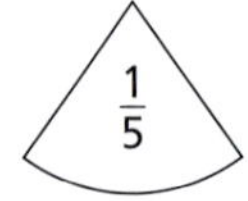

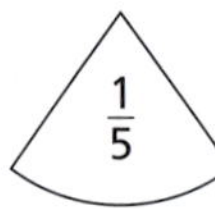

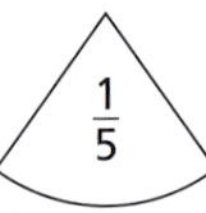

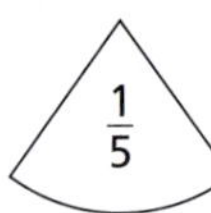

b. Bri writes $\frac{6}{1} \times \frac{1}{5}$.

c. Hiroshi writes 6×0.2.

47. Multiple Choice Linda is making bows to put on wreaths. Each bow uses $2\frac{1}{3}$ yards of ribbon. A spool of ribbon contains 15 yards of ribbon. Choose the number of whole bows she can make from one spool.

F. 6 **G.** 7 **H.** 12 **J.** 35

Extensions

48. Find each product.

a. $\frac{2}{3} \times \frac{1}{2} \times \frac{3}{4}$

b. $\frac{5}{8} \times \frac{1}{2} \times \frac{2}{3}$

49. Multiple Choice Choose the best answer for the number of square tiles needed to make a rectangle that is $4\frac{1}{3}$ tiles long by $\frac{1}{2}$ tile wide.

A. $2\frac{1}{3}$ **B.** $2\frac{1}{6}$ **C.** 2 **D.** $2\frac{1}{4}$

Mathematical Reflections 3

In this investigation, you explored situations that required you to multiply fractions. You also developed an algorithm for multiplying fractions. These questions will help you summarize what you have learned.

Think about your answers to these questions. Discuss your ideas with other students and your teacher. Then write a summary of your findings in your notebook.

1. Describe and illustrate your algorithm for multiplying fractions. Explain how you use the algorithm when you multiply fractions by fractions, fractions by mixed numbers, and fractions by whole numbers.
2. When you multiply two whole numbers, neither of which is zero, your answer is always equal to or greater than each of the factors. For example, $3 \times 5 = 15$, and 15 is greater than the factors 3 and 5. Use an example to help explain the following statement.

   When you multiply a fraction less than 1 by another fraction less than 1, your answer is always less than either factor.
3. Explain and illustrate what "of" means when you find a fraction *of* another number. What operation is implied by the word?

Investigation 4

Dividing With Fractions

In earlier investigations of this unit, you learned to use addition, subtraction, and multiplication of fractions in a variety of situations. There are times when you also need to divide fractions. To develop ideas about when and how to divide fractions, let's review the meaning of division in problems involving only whole numbers.

Getting Ready for Problem  4.1

Students at Lakeside Middle School raise funds to take a field trip each spring. In each of the following fundraising examples, explain how you recognize what operation(s) to use. Then write a number sentence to show the required calculations.

- The 24 members of the school swim team get dollar-per-mile pledges for a swim marathon they enter. The team goal is to swim 120 miles. How many miles should each swimmer swim?

- There are 360 students going on the field trip. Each school bus carries 30 students. How many buses are needed?
- The school band plans to sell 600 boxes of cookies. There are 20 members in the band. How many boxes should each member sell to reach the goal if each sells the same number of boxes?

Compare your number sentences and reasoning about these problems with classmates. Decide which are correct and why.

4.1 Preparing Food

There are times when the amounts given in a division situation are not whole numbers but fractions. First, you need to understand what division of fractions means. Then you can learn how to calculate quotients when the divisor or the dividend, or both, is a fraction.

When you do the division $12 \div 5$, what does the answer mean?

The answer should tell you how many fives are in 12 wholes. Because there is not a whole number of fives in 12, you might write:

$$12 \div 5 = 2\frac{2}{5}$$

Now the question is, what does the *fractional part* of the answer mean?

The answer means you can make 2 fives and $\frac{2}{5}$ *of another five.*

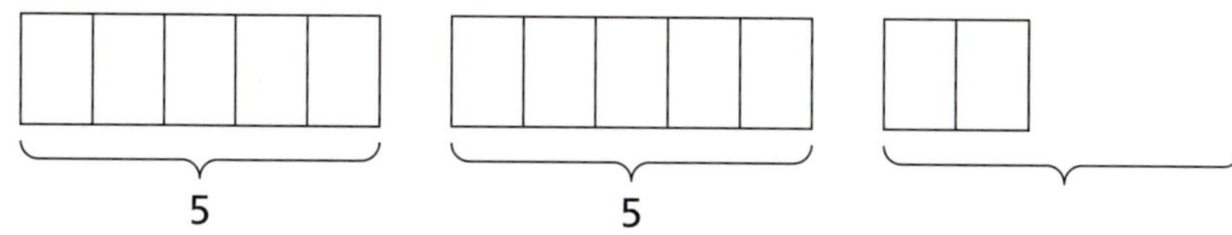

Suppose you ask, "How many $\frac{3}{4}$'s are in 14?" You can write this as a division problem, $14 \div \frac{3}{4}$.

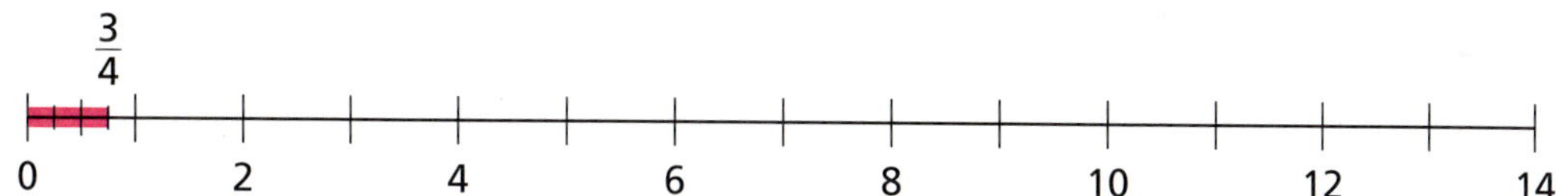

Can you make a whole number of $\frac{3}{4}$'s out of 14 wholes?

If not, what does the fractional part of the answer mean?

As you work through the problems in this investigation, keep these two questions in mind.

What does the answer to a division problem mean?

What does the fractional part of the answer to a division problem mean?

Problem 4.1 Dividing a Whole Number by a Fraction

Use written explanations or diagrams to show your reasoning for each part. Write a number sentence showing your calculation(s).

A. Naylah plans to make small cheese pizzas to sell at a school fundraiser. She has nine bars of cheese. How many pizzas can she make if each pizza needs the given amount of cheese?

1. $\frac{1}{3}$ bar **2.** $\frac{1}{4}$ bar **3.** $\frac{1}{5}$ bar

4. $\frac{1}{6}$ bar **5.** $\frac{1}{7}$ bar **6.** $\frac{1}{8}$ bar

B. Frank also has nine bars of cheese. How many pizzas can he make if each pizza needs the given amount of cheese?

1. $\frac{1}{3}$ bar **2.** $\frac{2}{3}$ bar **3.** $\frac{3}{3}$ bar **4.** $\frac{4}{3}$ bar

5. The answer to part (2) is a mixed number. What does the fractional part of the answer mean?

C. Use what you learned from Questions A and B to complete the following calculations.

1. $12 \div \frac{1}{3}$ **2.** $12 \div \frac{2}{3}$ **3.** $12 \div \frac{5}{3}$

4. $12 \div \frac{1}{6}$ **5.** $12 \div \frac{5}{6}$ **6.** $12 \div \frac{7}{6}$

7. The answer to part (3) is a mixed number. What does the fractional part of the answer mean in the context of cheese pizzas?

D. 1. Explain why $8 \div \frac{1}{3} = 24$ and $8 \div \frac{2}{3} = 12$.

2. Why is the answer to $8 \div \frac{2}{3}$ exactly half the answer to $8 \div \frac{1}{3}$?

E. Write an algorithm that seems to make sense for dividing any whole number by any fraction.

F. Write a story problem that can be solved using $12 \div \frac{2}{3}$. Explain why the calculation matches the story.

ACE **Homework starts on page 55.**

4.2 Fundraising Continues

While figuring prizes for the games at their fundraiser, students and teachers face more fraction problems!

Problem 4.2 Dividing a Fraction by a Whole Number

Use written explanations or diagrams to show your reasoning for each part. Write a number sentence showing your calculation(s).

A. Ms. Li brings peanuts to be shared equally by members of groups winning each game. How much of a pound of peanuts will each student get in the given situations?

1. Four students share $\frac{1}{2}$ pound of peanuts.
2. Three students share $\frac{1}{4}$ pound of peanuts.
3. Two students share $\frac{1}{5}$ pound of peanuts.

B. A popcorn store donates its different-sized boxes of popcorn for use as prizes at a team competition. How much popcorn does each team member get in the given situations?

1. A two-person team shares a $\frac{3}{4}$-pound box of popcorn equally.
2. A four-person team shares a $\frac{7}{8}$-pound box of popcorn equally.
3. A four-person team shares a $1\frac{1}{2}$-pound box of popcorn equally. (Remember $1\frac{1}{2} = \frac{3}{2}$.)

C. Find each quotient and explain which model you used.

1. $\frac{1}{2} \div 4$
2. $\frac{3}{2} \div 2$
3. $\frac{2}{5} \div 3$
4. $\frac{4}{5} \div 4$

D. What algorithm makes sense for dividing any fraction by any whole number?

E. Write a story problem that can be solved by $\frac{8}{3} \div 4$. Explain why the calculation matches the story.

ACE **Homework starts on page 55.**

4.3 Summer Work

In Problems 4.1 and 4.2, you developed ways of thinking about and solving division problems involving a whole number and a fraction. In the next problem, the questions involve division of a fraction by another fraction.

Problem 4.3 Dividing a Fraction by a Fraction

Rasheed and Ananda have summer jobs at a ribbon company. Answer the questions below. Use written explanations or diagrams in each to show your reasoning. Write a number sentence to show your calculation(s).

A. Rasheed takes a customer order for ribbon badges. It takes $\frac{1}{6}$ yard to make a ribbon for a badge. How many ribbon badges can he make from the given amounts of ribbon? Describe what each fractional part of an answer means.

1. $\frac{1}{2}$ yard

2. $\frac{3}{4}$ yard

3. $2\frac{2}{3}$ yards (Remember $2\frac{2}{3} = \frac{8}{3}$.)

B. Ananda is working on an order for bows. She uses $\frac{2}{3}$ yard of ribbon to make one bow. How many bows can Ananda make from each of the following amounts of ribbon?

1. $\frac{4}{5}$ yard **2.** $1\frac{3}{4}$ yards **3.** $2\frac{1}{3}$ yards

C. Solve each of the following examples as if they were ribbon problems.

1. $\frac{3}{4} \div \frac{2}{3}$ **2.** $1\frac{3}{4} \div \frac{1}{2}$ **3.** $2\frac{3}{4} \div \frac{3}{4}$

D. What algorithm makes sense for dividing any fraction by any fraction?

E. To solve $\frac{3}{4} \div \frac{2}{5}$, Elisha writes, "$\frac{3}{4} \div \frac{2}{5}$ is the same as $\frac{15}{20} \div \frac{8}{20}$. So the answer to $\frac{3}{4} \div \frac{2}{5}$ is the same as $15 \div 8$."

1. Is Elisha's first claim, that $\frac{3}{4} \div \frac{2}{5}$ is the same as $\frac{15}{20} \div \frac{8}{20}$, correct?

2. Is his second claim, that the answer to $\frac{3}{4} \div \frac{2}{5}$ is the same as $15 \div 8$, correct?

3. Use Elisha's method to solve $\frac{3}{5} \div \frac{1}{3}$. Does the method give a correct solution?

ACE **Homework starts on page 55.**

4.4 Writing a Division Algorithm

You are ready now to develop an algorithm for dividing fractions. To get started, you will break division problems into categories and write steps for each kind of problem. Then you can see whether there is one "big" algorithm that will solve them all.

Problem 4.4 Writing a Division Algorithm

A. 1. Find the quotients in each group below.

Group 1	Group 2	Group 3	Group 4
$\frac{1}{3} \div 9$	$12 \div \frac{1}{6}$	$\frac{5}{6} \div \frac{1}{12}$	$5 \div 1\frac{1}{2}$
$\frac{1}{6} \div 12$	$5 \div \frac{2}{3}$	$\frac{3}{4} \div \frac{3}{4}$	$\frac{1}{2} \div 3\frac{2}{3}$
$\frac{3}{5} \div 6$	$3 \div \frac{2}{5}$	$\frac{9}{5} \div \frac{1}{2}$	$3\frac{1}{3} \div \frac{2}{3}$

2. Describe what the problems in each group have in common.

3. Make up one new problem that fits in each group.

4. Write an algorithm that works for dividing *any* two fractions, including mixed numbers. Test your algorithm on the problems in the table. If necessary, change your algorithm until you think it will work all the time.

B. Use your algorithm to divide.

1. $9 \div \frac{4}{5}$ **2.** $1\frac{7}{8} \div 3$ **3.** $1\frac{2}{3} \div \frac{1}{5}$ **4.** $2\frac{5}{6} \div 1\frac{1}{3}$

C. Here is a multiplication-division fact family for whole numbers:

$5 \times 8 = 40$ $8 \times 5 = 40$ $40 \div 5 = 8$ $40 \div 8 = 5$

1. Complete this multiplication-division fact family for fractions.

$$\frac{2}{3} \times \frac{4}{5} = \frac{8}{15}$$

2. Check the division answers by using your algorithm.

D. For each number sentence, find a value for N that makes the sentence true. If needed, use fact families.

1. $\frac{2}{3} \div \frac{4}{5} = N$ **2.** $\frac{3}{4} \div N = \frac{7}{8}$ **3.** $N \div \frac{1}{4} = 3$

ACE **Homework starts on page 55.**

Applications Connections Extensions

Applications

1. The Easy Baking Company makes muffins. Some are small and some are huge. There are 20 cups of flour in the packages of flour they buy. How many muffins can be made from a package of flour if each takes the following amounts of flour?

a. $\frac{1}{4}$ cup **b.** $\frac{2}{4}$ cup **c.** $\frac{3}{4}$ cup

d. $\frac{1}{10}$ cup **e.** $\frac{2}{10}$ cup **f.** $\frac{7}{10}$ cup

g. $\frac{1}{7}$ cup **h.** $\frac{2}{7}$ cup **i.** $\frac{6}{7}$ cup

j. Explain how the answers for $20 \div \frac{1}{7}$, $20 \div \frac{2}{7}$, and $20 \div \frac{6}{7}$ are related. Show why this makes sense.

2. Find each quotient.

a. $6 \div \frac{3}{5}$ **b.** $5 \div \frac{2}{9}$ **c.** $3 \div \frac{1}{4}$ **d.** $4 \div \frac{5}{8}$

3. For parts (a)–(c), do the following steps:

- Draw pictures or write number sentences to show why your answer is correct.
- If there is a remainder, tell what the remainder means for the situation.

a. Bill is making 22 small pizzas for a party. He has 16 cups of flour. Each pizza crust takes $\frac{3}{4}$ cup of flour. Does he have enough flour?

b. There are 12 baby rabbits at the pet store. The manager lets Gabriella feed vegetables to the rabbits as treats. She has $5\frac{1}{4}$ ounces of parsley today. She wants to give each rabbit the same amount. How much parsley does each rabbit get?

c. It takes $18\frac{3}{8}$ inches of wood to make a frame for a small snapshot. Ms. Jones has 3 yards of wood. How many frames can she make?

4. Find each quotient. Describe any patterns that you see.

a. $5 \div \frac{1}{4}$ **b.** $5 \div \frac{1}{8}$ **c.** $5 \div \frac{1}{16}$

5. Maria uses $5\frac{1}{3}$ gallons of gas to drive to work and back four times.

a. How many gallons of gas does Maria use in one round trip to work?

b. Maria's car gets 28 miles to the gallon. How many miles is her round trip to work?

6. Anoki is in charge of giving prizes to teams at a mathematics competition. With each prize, he also wants to give each member of the team an equal amount of mints. How much will each team member get if Anoki has the given amounts of mints?

a. $\frac{1}{2}$ pound of mints for 8 students

b. $\frac{1}{4}$ pound of mints for 4 students

c. $\frac{3}{4}$ pound of mints for 3 students

d. $\frac{4}{5}$ pound of mints for 10 students

e. $1\frac{1}{2}$ pounds of mints for 2 students

7. Multiple Choice Nana's recipe for applesauce makes $8\frac{1}{2}$ cups. She serves the applesauce equally among her three grandchildren. How many cups of applesauce will each one get?

A. $\frac{3}{2}$ cups **B.** $25\frac{1}{2}$ cups **C.** $\frac{9}{6}$ cups **D.** Not here

8. Divide. Draw a picture to prove that each quotient makes sense.

a. $\frac{4}{5} \div 3$ **b.** $1\frac{2}{3} \div 5$ **c.** $\frac{5}{3} \div 5$

9. Multiple Choice Which of the following diagrams represents $4 \div \frac{1}{3}$?

F. 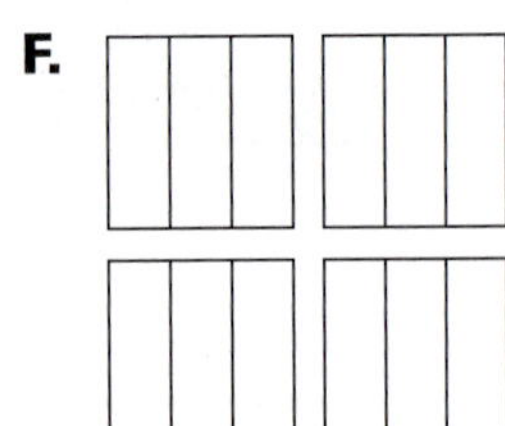

G. 

H. 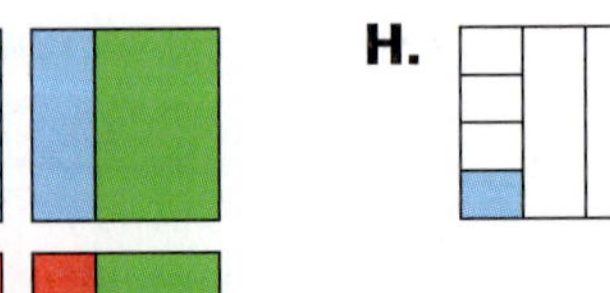

J. 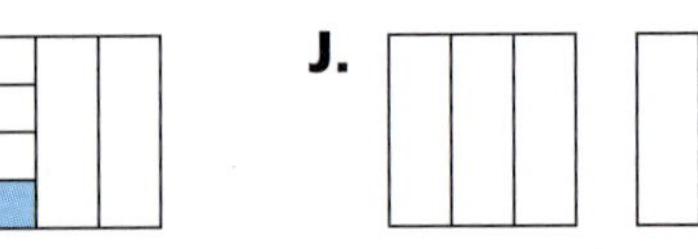

10. Multiple Choice Which of the following diagrams represents $\frac{1}{3} \div 4$?

A. 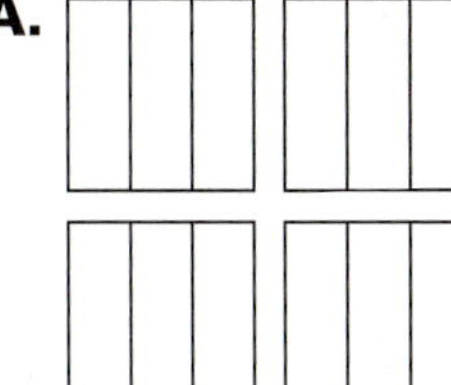

B. 

C. 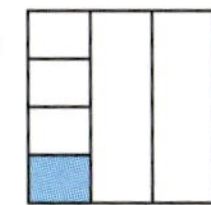

D. 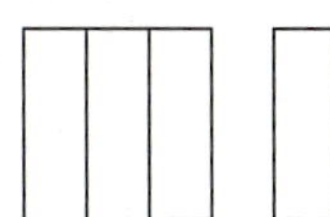

11. A latte (LAH tay) is the most popular coffee drink at Antonio's Coffee Shop.

Antonio makes only one size latte, and he uses $\frac{1}{3}$ cup of milk to make each drink. For parts (a)–(c), find:

- How many lattes he can make with the amount of milk given.
- What the remainder means, if there is one.

a. $\frac{7}{9}$ cup **b.** $\frac{5}{6}$ cup **c.** $3\frac{2}{3}$ cups

12. Write a story problem that can be solved using $1\frac{3}{4} \div \frac{1}{2}$. Explain why the calculation matches your story.

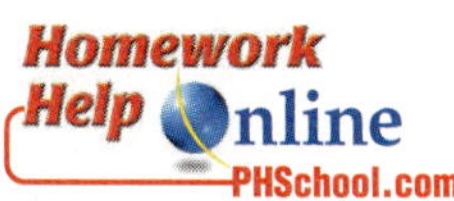

For: Help with Exercise 12
Web Code: ame-4412

13. Find each quotient.

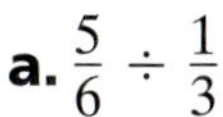

a. $\frac{5}{6} \div \frac{1}{3}$ **b.** $\frac{2}{3} \div \frac{1}{9}$ **c.** $1\frac{1}{2} \div \frac{3}{8}$

14. Is each quotient greater than or less than 1? Explain.

a. $\frac{7}{9} \div \frac{1}{9}$ **b.** $\frac{2}{3} \div \frac{1}{9}$ **c.** $\frac{1}{18} \div \frac{1}{9}$ **d.** $1 \div \frac{1}{9}$

Go Online
PHSchool.com
For: Multiple-Choice Skills Practice
Web Code: ama-4454

For Exercises 15–20, find the quotient.

15. $10 \div \frac{2}{3}$ **16.** $5 \div \frac{3}{4}$ **17.** $\frac{6}{7} \div 4$

18. $\frac{3}{10} \div 2$ **19.** $\frac{2}{5} \div \frac{1}{3}$ **20.** $2\frac{1}{2} \div 1\frac{1}{3}$

21. For Exercises 15 and 17 above, write a story problem to fit the computation.

Write a complete multiplication-division fact family.

22. $\frac{2}{3} \times \frac{5}{7} = \frac{10}{21}$ **23.** $\frac{3}{4} \div 1\frac{1}{2} = \frac{1}{2}$

Connections

24. Mr. Delgado jogs $2\frac{2}{5}$ km on a trail and then sits down to wait for his friend Mr. Prem. Mr. Prem has jogged $1\frac{1}{2}$ km down the trail. How much farther will Mr. Prem have to jog to reach Mr. Delgado?

25. Toshi has to work at the car wash for 3 hours. So far, he has worked $1\frac{3}{4}$ hours. How many more hours before he can leave work?

For Exercises 26–29, find each sum or difference. Then, give another fraction that is equivalent to the answer.

26. $\frac{9}{10} + \frac{1}{5}$ **27.** $\frac{5}{6} + \frac{7}{8}$ **28.** $\frac{2}{3} + 1\frac{1}{3}$ **29.** $12\frac{5}{6} - 8\frac{1}{4}$

30. Every fraction can be written in many equivalent forms. For example, $\frac{12}{15}$ is equivalent to $\frac{24}{30}$. For each fraction, find two equivalent fractions. One fraction should have a numerator greater than the one given. The other fraction should have a numerator less than the one given.

a. $\frac{4}{6}$ **b.** $\frac{10}{12}$ **c.** $\frac{12}{9}$ **d.** $\frac{8}{6}$

Find each product.

31. $\frac{2}{7} \times \frac{1}{3}$ **32.** $\frac{3}{4} \times \frac{7}{8}$ **33.** $1\frac{1}{2} \times \frac{1}{3}$ **34.** $4\frac{2}{3} \times 2\frac{3}{4}$

35. The marks on each number line are spaced so that the distance between two consecutive marks is the same. Copy each number line and label the marks.

a. 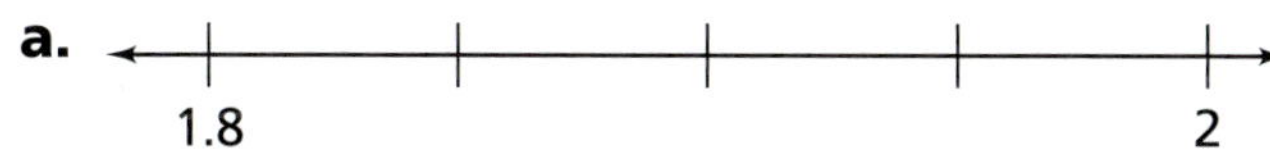

b. 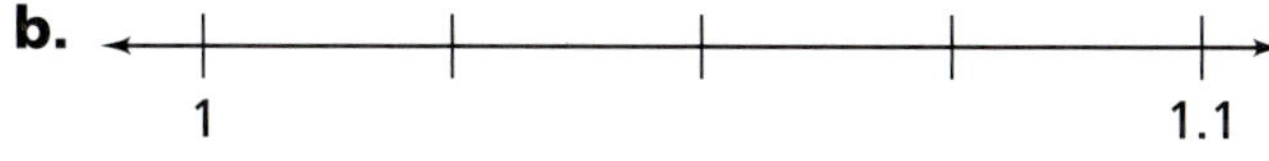

c. 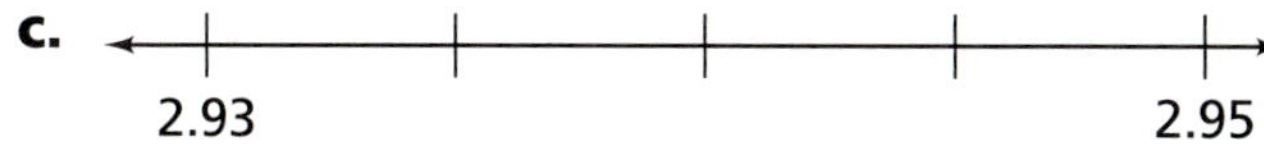

d. 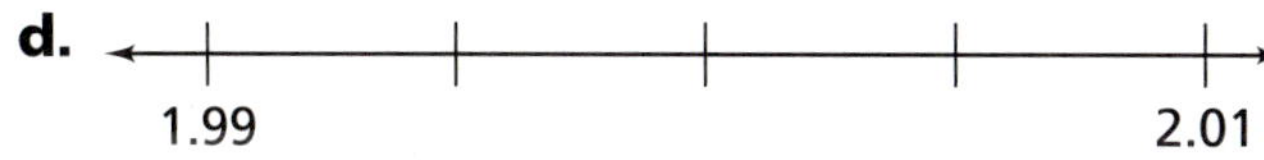

e. Explain how you determined what the labels should be.

36. By what number should you multiply to get 1 as the product?

a. $2 \times ■ = 1$ **b.** $\frac{1}{2} \times ■ = 1$ **c.** $3 \times ■ = 1$

d. $\frac{1}{3} \times ■ = 1$ **e.** $■ \times \frac{2}{3} = 1$ **f.** $\frac{3}{4} \times ■ = 1$

g. $■ \times \frac{5}{2} = 1$ **h.** $1\frac{1}{4} \times ■ = 1$ **i.** $\frac{7}{12} \times ■ = 1$

Applications Connections

37. Find the missing numbers in each pair. What is the relationship between each pair?

a. $3 \div ■ = 9$

$3 \times ■ = 9$

b. $3 \div ■ = 12$

$3 \times ■ = 12$

c. $2\frac{1}{2} \div ■ = 5$

$2\frac{1}{2} \times ■ = 5$

38. Use the cartoon to answer the questions below.

a. How many slices of the pizza will have olives?

b. How many slices of the pizza will be plain?

c. What fraction of the pizza will have onions and green peppers?

Extensions

39. DonTae says that when you want to find out how many quarters are in some whole number of dollars, you should divide the number of dollars by $\frac{1}{4}$. Vanna says that you need to multiply the number of dollars by 4. With whom do you agree? Why?

40. Find a value for N that makes the sentence true. Don't forget fact families.

a. $N \times \frac{1}{5} = \frac{2}{15}$

b. $N \div \frac{1}{5} = \frac{2}{3}$

c. $\frac{1}{2} \times N = \frac{1}{3}$

d. $\frac{1}{5} \div N = \frac{1}{3}$

e. $1\frac{3}{4} \div N = \frac{1}{4}$

f. $2\frac{2}{3} \div N = 8$

41. Use the table below to solve parts (a)–(e).

Measurement	Equivalent Measurement
1 cup	16 tablespoons
1 quart	4 cups
1 quart	2 pints
1 gallon	4 quarts
1 tablespoon	3 teaspoons

a. Brian is missing his measuring cup. He needs to measure out $\frac{1}{2}$ cup of vegetable oil. How many tablespoons should he use?

b. How many teaspoons does Brian need to use to measure out $\frac{1}{2}$ cup of vegetable oil?

c. What fraction of a quart is $\frac{1}{2}$ cup?

d. What fraction of a gallon is $\frac{1}{2}$ cup?

e. Suppose you need to measure out exactly one gallon of water. The only measuring cups you have are $\frac{1}{2}$ cup, 1 cup, and 1 pint. Which measuring cup would you use? How would you make sure you had exactly one gallon?

Connections Extensions

Mathematical Reflections 4

In this investigation, you developed strategies for dividing with fractions. You developed algorithms that can be used to divide any two fractions or mixed numbers. These questions will help you to summarize what you have learned.

Think about your answers to these questions. Discuss your ideas with other students and your teacher. Then write a summary of your findings in your notebook.

1. Explain your algorithm for dividing two fractions. Demonstrate your algorithm with an example for each situation.
   - a whole number divided by a fraction
   - a fraction divided by a whole number
   - a fraction divided by a fraction
   - a mixed number divided by a fraction
2. Explain why the following example can be solved using division.

   A local coffee house donates $2\frac{2}{3}$ pounds of gourmet coffee beans to be sold at a local fundraiser. The people running the fundraiser decide to package and sell the coffee beans in $\frac{1}{2}$-pound packages. How many $\frac{1}{2}$-pound packages can they make?
3. How is the quotient of $20 \div \frac{1}{5}$ related to the quotient of $20 \div \frac{3}{5}$? Explain.

Looking Back and Looking Ahead

Unit Review

The problems in this unit helped you develop strategies for estimating and computing with fractions. You learned how to identify situations that call for computation with fractions. You developed algorithms for adding, subtracting, multiplying, and dividing fractions. You learned how to solve problems with fractions. Use what you have learned to solve the following examples.

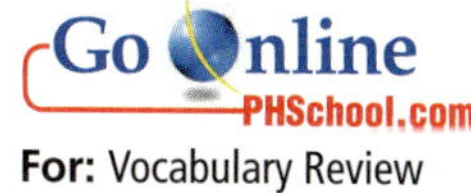

For: Vocabulary Review Puzzle
Web Code: amj-4051

Use Your Understanding: Fraction Operations

1. The Scoop Shop sells many types of nuts. Jayne asks for this mix:

$\frac{1}{2}$ pound peanuts
$\frac{1}{6}$ pound hazelnuts
$\frac{1}{3}$ pound almonds
$\frac{3}{4}$ pound cashews
$\frac{1}{4}$ pound pecans

a. Nuts cost $5.00 per pound. What is Jayne's bill?

b. What fraction of the mix does each kind of nut represent?

c. Diego does not like cashews, so he asks for Jayne's mix without the cashews. What is his bill?

d. Kalli is making small bowls of nuts for a party. Each bowl uses $\frac{1}{4}$ cup of nuts. Kalli has $3\frac{3}{8}$ cups of nuts. How many bowls can she make?

2. Shaquille likes dried fruit. He wants a mix of peaches, cherries, pineapple chunks, and apple rings. The following chart shows how much The Scoop Shop has of each fruit and how much of each fruit Shaquille orders.

The Scoop Shop's Stock	Shaquille's Order
$1\frac{1}{2}$ pounds dried peaches	$\frac{1}{3}$ of the stock
$\frac{4}{5}$ pound dried cherries	$\frac{1}{2}$ of the stock
$\frac{3}{4}$ pound dried pineapple chunks	$\frac{2}{3}$ of the stock
$2\frac{1}{4}$ pounds dried apple rings	$\frac{3}{5}$ of the stock

a. How many pounds of dried fruit does Shaquille order?

b. Dried fruit cost $5.00 per pound. What is Shaquille's bill?

Explain Your Reasoning

When you use mathematical calculations to solve a problem or make a decision, it is important to be able to support each step in your reasoning.

3. What operations did you use to find the cost of the nuts in Jayne's mix?

4. How did you find the fraction of the mix for each kind of nut?

5. $4 \div \frac{1}{3} = 12$ and $4 \div \frac{2}{3} = 6$. Why is the second answer half of the first?

6. Use the following problems to show the steps involved in algorithms for adding, subtracting, multiplying, and dividing fractions. Be prepared to explain your reasoning.

a. $\frac{5}{6} + \frac{1}{4}$ **b.** $\frac{3}{4} - \frac{2}{3}$ **c.** $\frac{2}{5} \times \frac{3}{8}$ **d.** $\frac{3}{8} \div \frac{3}{4}$

Look Ahead

The ideas and techniques you have used in this unit will be applied and expanded in future units of *Connected Mathematics*, in other mathematics work in school, and in your future work. Fractions are used in measuring and calculating quantities of all kinds—from length, area, and volume to time, money, test scores, and weights.

English / Spanish Glossary

A

algorithm A set of rules for performing a procedure. Mathematicians invent algorithms that are useful in many kinds of situations. Some examples of algorithms are the rules for long division or the rules for adding two fractions. The following algorithm was written by a middle-grade student:

To add two fractions, first change them to equivalent fractions with the same denominator. Then add the numerators and put the sum over the common denominator.

algoritmo Un conjunto de reglas para realizar un procedimiento. Los matemáticos inventan algoritmos que son útiles en muchos tipos de situaciones. Algunos ejemplos de algoritmos son las reglas para una división larga o las reglas para sumar dos fracciones. El siguiente es un algoritmo escrito por un estudiante de un grado intermedio.

Para sumar dos fracciones, primero transfórmalas en fracciones equivalentes con el mismo denominador. Luego suma los numeradores y coloca la suma sobre el denominador común.

B

benchmark A "nice" number that can be used to estimate the size of other numbers. For work with fractions, 0, $\frac{1}{2}$, and 1 are good benchmarks. We often estimate fractions or decimals with benchmarks because it is easier to do arithmetic with them, and estimates often give enough accuracy for the situation. For example, many fractions and decimals—such as $\frac{37}{50}$, $\frac{5}{8}$, 0.43, and 0.55—can be thought of as being close to $\frac{1}{2}$. You might say $\frac{5}{8}$ is between $\frac{1}{2}$ and 1 but closer to $\frac{1}{2}$, so you can estimate $\frac{5}{8}$ to be about $\frac{1}{2}$. We also use benchmarks to help compare fractions. For example, we could say that $\frac{5}{8}$ is greater than 0.43 because $\frac{5}{8}$ is greater than $\frac{1}{2}$ and 0.43 is less than $\frac{1}{2}$.

punto de referencia Un número "bueno" que se puede usar para estimar el tamaño de otros números. Para trabajar con fracciones, 0, $\frac{1}{2}$ y 1 son buenos puntos de referencia. Por lo general estimamos fracciones o decimales con puntos de referencia porque nos resulta más fácil hacer cálculos aritméticos con ellos, y las estimaciones suelen ser bastante exactas para la situación. Por ejemplo, muchas fracciones y decimales, como por ejemplo $\frac{37}{50}$, $\frac{5}{8}$, 0.43 y 0.55, se pueden considerar como cercanos a $\frac{1}{2}$. Se podría decir que $\frac{5}{8}$ está entre $\frac{1}{2}$ y 1, pero más cerca de $\frac{1}{2}$, por lo que se puede estimar que $\frac{5}{8}$ es alrededor de $\frac{1}{2}$. También usamos puntos de referencia para ayudarnos a comparar fracciones. Por ejemplo, podríamos decir que $\frac{5}{8}$ es mayor que 0.43, porque $\frac{5}{8}$ es mayor que $\frac{1}{2}$ y 0.43 es menor que $\frac{1}{2}$.

denominator The number written below the line in a fraction. In the fraction $\frac{3}{4}$, 4 is the denominator. In the part-whole interpretation of fractions, the denominator shows the number of equal-sized parts into which the whole has been split.

denominador El número escrito debajo de la línea en una fracción. En la fracción $\frac{3}{4}$, 4 es el denominador. En la interpretación de partes y enteros de fracciones, el denominador muestra el número de partes iguales en que fue dividido el entero.

E

equivalent fractions Fractions that are equal in value, but may have different numerators and denominators. For example, $\frac{2}{3}$ and $\frac{14}{21}$ are equivalent fractions. The shaded part of this rectangle represents both $\frac{2}{3}$ and $\frac{14}{21}$

fracciones equivalentes Fracciones de igual valor, que pueden tener diferentes numeradores y denominadores. Por ejemplo, $\frac{2}{3}$ y $\frac{14}{21}$ son fracciones equivalentes. La parte sombreada de este rectángulo representa tanto $\frac{2}{3}$ como $\frac{14}{21}$.

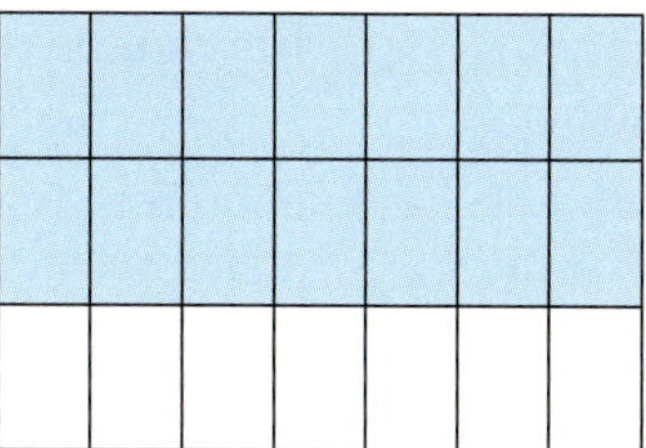

F

fact family A set of related addition-subtraction sentences or multiplication-division sentences. For example, the set of numbers 3, 5, and 15 are part of this multiplication-division fact family:

$3 \times 5 = 15$ $5 \times 3 = 15$
$15 \div 5 = 3$ $15 \div 3 = 5$

If you have one fact from a family, you can use the addition-subtraction or multiplication-division relationship to write the three related facts that are also part of the family. For example, with $2 + 3 = 5$, you can use the relationship between addition and subtraction to write the related number sentences $3 + 2 = 5$, $5 - 3 = 2$, and $5 - 2 = 3$.

familia de datos Conjunto de oraciones de suma y resta o de multiplicación y división relacionadas. Por ejemplo, el grupo de números 3, 5 y 15 son parte de esta familia de datos de multiplicación y división:

$3 \times 5 = 15$ $5 \times 3 = 15$
$15 \div 5 = 3$ $15 \div 3 = 5$

Si tienes un dato de una familia, puedes usar la relación entre la suma y la resta, y entre la multiplicación y división para escribir los tres datos relacionados que también son parte de la familia. Por ejemplo, con $2 + 3 = 5$, puedes usar la relación entre la suma y la resta para escribir las oraciones numéricas relacionadas $3 + 2 = 5$, $5 - 3 = 2$ y $5 - 2 = 3$.

N

numerator The number written above the line in a fraction. In the fraction $\frac{5}{8}$, 5 is the numerator. When you interpret the fraction $\frac{5}{8}$ as a part of a whole, the numerator 5 tells that the fraction refers to 5 of the 8 equal parts.

numerador El número escrito sobre la línea en una fracción. En la fracción $\frac{5}{8}$, 5 es el numerador. Cuando interpretas una fracción como $\frac{5}{8}$ como parte de un entero, el numerador 5 te dice que la fracción se refiere a 5 de 8 partes iguales.

R

reciprocal A factor by which you multiply a given number so that their product is 1. For example, $\frac{3}{5}$ is the reciprocal of $\frac{5}{3}$, and $\frac{5}{3}$ is the reciprocal of $\frac{3}{5}$ because $\frac{3}{5} \times \frac{5}{3} = 1$. Note that the reciprocal of $1\frac{2}{3}$ is $\frac{3}{5}$ because $1\frac{2}{3} \times \frac{3}{5} = 1$.

número recíproco Un factor por el cual multiplicas un número dado de manera que su producto sea 1. Por ejemplo, $\frac{3}{5}$ es el número recíproco de $\frac{5}{3}$, y $\frac{5}{3}$ es el número recíproco de $\frac{3}{5}$, porque $\frac{3}{5} \times \frac{5}{3} = 1$. Fíjate que el recíproco de $1\frac{2}{3}$ es $\frac{3}{5}$, porque $1\frac{2}{3} \times \frac{3}{5} = 1$.

U

unit fraction A fraction with a numerator of 1. For example, in the unit fraction $\frac{1}{13}$, the part-whole interpretation of fractions tells us that the whole has been split into 13 equal-sized parts, and that the fraction represents the quantity of 1 of those parts.

fracción de unidad Una fracción con numerador 1. Por ejemplo, en la fracción de unidad $\frac{1}{13}$, la interpretación de fracciones de una parte entera nos indica que el entero ha sido dividido en 13 partes iguales y que la fracción representa la cantidad 1 de esas partes.

Academic Vocabulary

The following terms are important to your understanding of the mathematics in this unit. Knowing and using these words will help you in thinking, reasoning, representing, communicating your ideas, and making connections across ideas. When these words make sense to you, the investigations and problems will make more sense as well.

E

explain To give facts and details that make an idea easier to understand. Explaining can involve a written summary supported by a diagram, chart, table, or a combination of these.

related terms: analyze, clarify, describe, justify, tell

Sample: Explain why the answer to $12 \div \frac{3}{4}$ is one third the answer to $12 \div \frac{1}{4}$.

> Because $\frac{3}{4} = 3 \times \frac{1}{4}$, it takes three $\frac{1}{4}$s to make every $\frac{3}{4}$. There are forty-eight $\frac{1}{4}$s in 12, but there are only sixteen $\frac{3}{4}$s in 12.

explicar Dar hechos y detalles que hacen que una idea sea más fácil de comprender. Explicar puede implicar un resumen escrito apoyado por un diagrama, una gráfica, una tabla o una combinación de éstos.

términos relacionados: analizar, aclarar, describir, justificar, decir

Ejemplo: Explica por qué la respuesta a $12 \div \frac{3}{4}$ es un tercio de la respuesta a $12 \div \frac{1}{4}$.

> Porque $\frac{3}{4} = 3 \times \frac{1}{4}$, se requieren tres $\frac{1}{4}$ para formar cada $\frac{3}{4}$. Hay cuarenta y ocho $\frac{1}{4}$ en 12, pero sólo hay dieciséis $\frac{3}{4}$ en 12.

M

model To represent a situation using pictures, diagrams, or number sentences.

related terms: represent, demonstrate

Sample: Yolanda has one half of an apple pie. She eats one third of the half pie. Model this situation using a number sentence or a picture.

> I can write one third as $\frac{1}{3}$ and half as $\frac{1}{2}$, so one third of one half can be written as $\frac{1}{3} \times \frac{1}{2}$. Because $\frac{1}{3} \times \frac{1}{2} = \frac{1}{6}$, she eats $\frac{1}{6}$ of the entire pie.
> I can also divide a whole fraction strip into halves, then divide each half into thirds.

$\frac{1}{2}$			$\frac{1}{2}$		
$\frac{1}{6}$	$\frac{1}{6}$	$\frac{1}{6}$	$\frac{1}{6}$	$\frac{1}{6}$	$\frac{1}{6}$

> Yolanda eats $\frac{1}{6}$ of the entire pie.

hacer modelos Representar una situación usando imágenes, diagramas u oraciones numéricas.

términos relacionados: representar, demostrar

Ejemplo: Yolanda tiene una mitad de una tarta de manzana. Se come un tercio de la mitad de la tarta. Haz un modelo de esta situación usando una oración numérica o una imagen.

> Puedo escribir un tercio como $\frac{1}{3}$ y la mitad como $\frac{1}{2}$, así que un tercio de una mitad puede escribirse como $\frac{1}{3} \times \frac{1}{2}$. Debido a que $\frac{1}{3} \times \frac{1}{2} = \frac{1}{6}$, ella se come $\frac{1}{6}$ de la tarta entera.
> También puedo dividir una tira de fracciones entera en mitades, luego divido cada mitad en tercios.

$\frac{1}{2}$			$\frac{1}{2}$		
$\frac{1}{6}$	$\frac{1}{6}$	$\frac{1}{6}$	$\frac{1}{6}$	$\frac{1}{6}$	$\frac{1}{6}$

> Yolanda se come $\frac{1}{6}$ de la tarta entera.

R

reason To think through using facts and information.
related terms: *think, examine, logic*

Sample: **To find the number of $\frac{1}{2}$-cup servings in 6 cups, Jenni says it is necessary to multiply 6 by $\frac{1}{2}$. Zach says that 6 must be divided by $\frac{1}{2}$ to find the number of servings. With whom do you agree? Explain how you reasoned.**

> I agree with Zach because you want to know how many halves there are in 6. This question is answered by division: $6 \div \frac{1}{2} = 12$. Multiplying 6 by $\frac{1}{2}$ separates it into 2 equal parts of 3 each. That is not what is asked for in the question.

razonar Considerar usando hechos e información.
términos relacionados: *pensar, examinar, lógica*

Ejemplo: **Para hallar el número de porciones de $\frac{1}{2}$ taza en 6 tazas, Jenni dice que es necesario multiplicar 6 por $\frac{1}{2}$. Zach dice que 6 debe dividirse entre $\frac{1}{2}$ para hallar el número de porciones. ¿Con quién estás de acuerdo? Explica cómo hiciste tu razonamiento.**

> Estoy de acuerdo con Zach porque se desea saber cuántas mitades hay en 6. Esta pregunta se responde por división: $6 \div \frac{1}{2} = 12$. Multiplicar 6 por $\frac{1}{2}$ lo separa en 2 partes iguales de 3 cada una. Esto no es lo que se pide en la pregunta.

recall To remember a fact quickly.
related terms: *remember, recognize*

Sample: **Mateo wants to add 0.3 to $\frac{1}{2}$. What can you recall about $\frac{1}{2}$ or 0.3 that will help him find the sum? Explain.**

> I recall that $\frac{1}{2}$ is equivalent to the decimal 0.5. When both numbers are in decimal form, they can be added easily. Mateo can add $0.5 + 0.3$ to get 0.8.
>
> I also recall that 0.3 is the same as $\frac{3}{10}$ and $\frac{1}{2}$ is equivalent to $\frac{5}{10}$. Mateo can add $\frac{3}{10} + \frac{5}{10}$ to get $\frac{8}{10}$ which is the same as 0.8.

recordar Acordarse rápido de un hecho.
términos relacionados: *acordarse, reconocer*

Ejemplo: **Mateo desea sumar 0.3 a $\frac{1}{2}$. ¿Qué puedes recordar sobre $\frac{1}{2}$ o 0.3 que le ayudará a hallar la suma? Explica tu respuesta.**

> Recuerdo que $\frac{1}{2}$ es equivalente al decimal 0.5. Cuando ambos números están en forma decimal, pueden sumarse con facilidad. Mateo puede sumar $0.5 + 0.3$ para obtener 0.8.
>
> También recuerdo que 0.3 is igual a $\frac{3}{10}$ y $\frac{1}{2}$ es equivalente a $\frac{5}{10}$. Mateo puede sumar $\frac{3}{10} + \frac{5}{10}$ para obtener $\frac{8}{10}$, que es igual a 0.8.

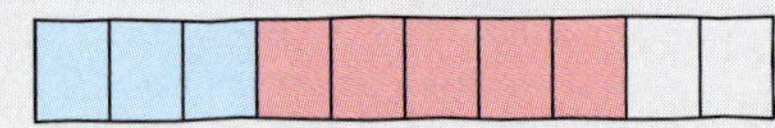

Index

Acting it out, 6–7

Addition
- ACE, 10–12, 24–30, 46, 58
- algorithm, 22–23, 64
- estimation, 5–9, 10–12, 15
- of fractions, 8–9, 10–12, 16–23, 24–30, 31, 46, 58

Adjacent 18

Algebra
- algorithm 22, 23, 35, 39, 43, 47, 50 51, 53, 54, 62, 64
- difference 4, 23, 25, 46, 59
- dividend 49
- divisor 49
- equivalent 4, 9, 12,14, 16, 26, 28, 37, 38, 59
- inverse 4
- number line 12, 30, 49, 59
- operation 4, 33, 47, 63, 64
- plot 30
- point 12
- product 4, 35, 37, 39–42, 46, 59
- quotient 4, 49, 51, 54–58, 62
- reciprocal 39
- set 13, 29
- solution 4, 18, 27, 53
- solve 28, 35, 53
- sum 4, 7–10, 23, 25, 26, 46, 59

Algorithm, 65
- for adding fractions, 22–23, 64
- for dividing fractions, 50–51, 53–54, 62, 64
- for multiplying fractions, 35, 38–39, 43, 47, 64
- for subtracting fractions, 22–23, 64

Area model, 18, 49, 66
- ACE, 24–25, 27–28, 46, 56–57

Benchmark
- ACE, 10–12, 26
- decimal, 5, 10–12, 65
- fraction, 4, 5–7, 10–12, 26, 65
- percent, 12

Check for reasonableness, 4, 9, 36–38, 54
- ACE, 55–56

Compare decimals, 10, 28

Compare fractions, 5–7, 19
- ACE, 10, 24–25, 40, 44, 57

Concrete model, *see* Model

Decimals
- ACE, 10–13, 28
- benchmarks, 5, 10–12, 65
- comparing, 10, 28
- equivalent, 12
- estimating with, 5–7, 10–11, 15
- fractions and, 5–7, 10–12
- ordering, 13

Denominator, 66

Dividend 49

Division
- ACE, 55–61
- algorithm, 50–51, 53–54, 62, 64
- reasonableness, 54–56
- with fractions, 45, 48–54, 55–61, 62

Divisor 49

Drawing a picture, 33, 35–36, 38, 51
- ACE, 12–13, 28, 40, 56

Equivalent 4, 9, 12,14, 16, 26, 28, 37, 38, 59

Estimation
- ACE, 10–14
- overestimating, 8–9, 15
- underestimating, 8–9, 15
- with decimals, 5–7, 10–11, 15
- with fractions, 5–9, 10–14, 15, 33, 35–38, 41

Fact families, 4, 21–22, 31, 54, 66
- ACE, 26, 45, 58, 60

Fraction strips, 14, 27

Fractions
- ACE, 10–14, 24–30, 40–46, 55–61
- adding, 8–9, 10–12, 16–23, 24–30, 31, 46, 58
- addition and subtraction algorithms for, 22–23, 64
- benchmarks, 4, 5–7, 10, 26
- comparing, 5–7, 10, 19, 24–25, 40, 44, 57
- decimals and, 5–7, 10–12
- division, 45, 48–54, 55–61, 62
- equivalent, 9, 12–14, 21, 27–28, 38, 46, 58, 66
- estimating with, 5–9, 10–14, 15
- and fraction strips, 14, 27
- multiplication algorithm for, 35, 38–39, 43, 47, 64
- multiplying, 32–39, 40–46, 47
- subtracting, 16, 20–23, 24–30, 31, 46, 58
- unit, 67

Getting Close game, 5–7
- ACE, 10
- Getting Even Closer, 10
- rules, 6

Interpreting data
- area model, 18, 24–25, 27–28, 46, 49, 56–57, 66
- fraction strips, 14, 27
- game cards, 6–7
- number line, 12, 14, 30, 49, 59
- percent bar, 34
- picture, 6–7, 12–13, 20, 33, 44, 46, 55, 56–57, 59–60
- table, 23, 39, 45, 54, 61
- thermometer, *see* percent bar

Interval 14, 26

Inverse 4

Investigations
- Adding and Subtracting Fractions, 16–31
- Estimating With Fractions, 5–15
- Multiplying With Fractions, 32–47
- Dividing With Fractions, 48–62

Justify or explain method, 8–9, 15, 22, 31, 35, 37–38, 48, 51, 53, 62, 64
- ACE, 10, 13, 60

Justify or explain solution (*see also* Check for reasonableness), 15, 22, 35, 49–50, 53
- ACE, 10–11, 24, 26, 29, 41, 45–46, 55, 57, 59

Looking Back and Looking Ahead: Unit Reflections, 63–64

Looking for a pattern, 4, 23, 35, 39, 54
ACE, 26, 40, 42, 56, 59

Manipulatives
game cards, 6–7

Mathematical Highlights, 4

Mathematical Reflections, 15, 31, 47, 62

Model
area, 18, 24–25, 27–28, 35, 40, 46, 49, 56–57, 66
fraction strips, 14, 27
number line, 12, 14, 30, 34–35, 49, 59
percent bar, 34
picture, 6–7, 12–13, 20, 33, 44, 46, 55, 56–57, 59–60
thermometer, *see* percent bar

Multiplication
ACE, 40–46, 58–60
algorithm, 35, 38–39, 43, 47, 64
with fractions, 32–39, 40–46, 47, 58–60
pattern, 35, 38–39, 40, 42
reasonable answers, 36–38

Notebook, 15, 31, 47, 62

Number line
ACE, 12, 30, 59
drawing, 12, 30, 34–35, 59
interpreting, 12, 14, 30, 49, 59

Numerator, 67

Order decimals, 13

Order fractions, 5, 14

Percent
benchmarks, 12
equivalent, 12

Percent bar, 34

Pictorial model, *see* Model

Plot 30

Point 12

Problem-solving strategies
acting it out, 6–7
drawing a number line, 12, 30, 34–35, 59
drawing a picture, 12–13, 28, 33, 35–36, 38, 40, 51, 56
looking for a pattern, 4, 23, 26, 35, 39, 40, 42, 54, 56, 59

Product 4, 35, 37, 39–42, 46, 59

Quotient 4, 49, 51, 54–58, 62

Reasonableness, *see* Check for reasonableness

Reciprocal, 39, 67

Set 13, 29

Solution 4, 18, 27, 53

Solve 28, 35, 53

Subtraction
ACE, 24–30, 46, 58
algorithm, 22–23, 64
with fractions, 16, 20–23, 24–30, 31, 46, 58

Sum 4, 7–10, 23, 25, 26, 46, 59

Thermometer, *see* percent bar

Acknowledgments

Team Credits

The people who made up the **Connected Mathematics2** team—representing editorial, editorial services, design services, and production services—are listed below. Bold type denotes core team members.

Leora Adler, Judith Buice, Kerry Cashman, Patrick Culleton, Sheila DeFazio, Richard Heater, **Barbara Hollingdale, Jayne Holman,** Karen Holtzman, **Etta Jacobs,** Christine Lee, Carolyn Lock, Catherine Maglio, **Dotti Marshall,** Rich McMahon, Eve Melnechuk, Kristin Mingrone, Terri Mitchell, **Marsha Novak,** Irene Rubin, Donna Russo, Robin Samper, Siri Schwartzman, **Nancy Smith,** Emily Soltanoff, **Mark Tricca,** Paula Vergith, Roberta Warshaw, Helen Young

Additional Credits

Diana Bonfilio, Mairead Reddin, Michael Torocsik, nSight, Inc.

Technical Illustration

WestWords, Inc.

Cover Design

tom white.images

Photos

2 t, Courtesy of JCL Equipment Co. Inc.; **2 b,** GK Hart/Vikki Hart/Getty Images, Inc.; **3,** Ed Young/Corbis; **7,** Richard Haynes; **8,** Syracuse Newspapers/The Image Works; **17,** PhotoDisc/PictureQuest; **19,** Paul Hardy/Corbis; **22,** Richard Haynes; **29,** E.R. Degginger/Bruce Coleman, Inc.; **32,** Richard Haynes; **35,** Courtesy of JCL Equipment Co. Inc.; **37,** Russ Lappa; **41,** L. Clarke/Corbis; **43,** Tony Freeman/PhotoEdit; **48,** Tony Freeman/PhotoEdit; **51 l,** Dorling Kindersley; **51 r,** Royalty-Free/Corbis; **52,** Ed Scott/AGE Fotostock; **55,** GK Hart/Vikki Hart/Getty Images, Inc.; **58,** Eric Bean/Getty Images, Inc.; **60,** ©2001, Hilary B. Price. Distributed by King Features Syndicate, Inc.; **61,** Silver Burdett Ginn; **63,** Russ Lappa